BELIEVE, PLUS NOTHING

By

DR. W. O. VAUGHT, JR.

Erma portis:

I trust the doctrine in
this book will be a
blessing to you.
My friendship
W. O. Vaught

CONTENTS

DEDICATION

To Mary Frances, my companion across the years;
To Carl Gray, our son, Head of the Philosophy Department at Penn State University;
And to my dear members of Immanuel Baptist Church, Little Rock, Arkansas, where the doctrine in this book has been preached.

PREFACE

The material in this book has been coming into focus in my mind for about a dozen years. This book is not sent forth to be read casually as one reads a story or novel. In order for this doctrine to become real in the reader's mind, it will have to be studied carefully. It can best be studied with the Bible open and it is my hope that when Scripture is referred to, the reader will look up the passage in the Bible and study it until the message becomes vital and real.

About a dozen years ago, I decided to turn from what is known as "topical preaching" to word by word and line by line preaching. As a result of this experience, the Bible became a new book to me, and truth began to leap out of its pages. I intensified my study habits and began to spend the major portion of every day in meditation and study. I discovered from passages like 1 Corinthians 2:16 that the Bible is the mind of Christ. I had always had a great reverence and love for the Word of God, but with this new experience, the Bible came to have first place in my life and thought. One verse in the Bible became the centerpiece of my thinking: "For the word of God is alive and powerful, sharper than any two-edged sword, piercing even to the dividing asunder of the soul and the spirit, and of the joints and the marrow and is a discerner of the thoughts and the intents of the heart" (Hebrews 4:12). In addition, 2 Timothy 2:15 became the driving force of my daily schedule: "Study to show thyself approved unto God, a workman that needeth not to be ashamed, rightly dividing the word of truth." The last phrase of that scripture, "cutting straight the word of truth," were the Greek words I read carved above the entrance of Norton Hall at the Southern Baptist Seminary, where I spent my student days. Little did I know then what those Greek words would come to mean to me later.

There is another line from the Apostle Paul which began to burn in my mind at this time and which lays the foundation for the task of exposition of the scripture: "All scripture is God breathed and is profitable for doctrine, for reproof, for correction, for instruction in righteousness: that the man of God may be mature, thoroughly furnished unto all good works" (2 Timothy 3:16-17).

For many years I had been seeking to do the will of God. I heard the late Mrs. J. M. Dawson of Waco, Texas, quote the world famous George W. Truett in these words —

"To know the will of God is the greatest knowledge;
To find the will of God is the greatest discovery;
To do the will of God is the greatest achievement."

But in the course of my daily studies I came to discover that you cannot

i

know the Will of God unless you know the Word of God, for it is in the Word of God that the Will of God is revealed. I discovered a heart hunger here in my church for a careful and accurate interpretation of the Word of God. This quest has been going on now for more than a dozen years, and the material in this book will reveal the heart of what has been discovered.

I do not contend that I will make a full sweep of Christian Theology in this book, but rather, I am writing for the earnest Christian student who wants to know the truth of how to live the Christian life. I believe a great deal of false teaching has grown up around the ideas of the nature of God, salvation, the meaning of faith in Christ, eternal security and other major doctrines which lead to a triumphant life in Christ. It is to these fundamental issues that I wish to address myself in the following pages.

While the material of this book was being crystallized in my mind, I was holding a Bible Conference in one of our southern towns. A wealthy and successful businessman called my motel room and asked me to visit with him. During our conversation I discovered that he had been listening to my Sunday morning messages on television for about five years. He related some of the experiences of his early life and then told me how he had come to have certainty and assurance concerning his salvation. He said, "The morning you preached your sermon, *Believe, Plus Nothing,* was the morning I came to know Christ with absolute assurance." In that instant God gave me the title for this book, and for this reason, I am confident that "Believe, Plus Nothing" will form one of the most significant chapters in this unfolding story.

I am indebted to my Christian parents who first introduced me to the doctrine in this book, by living these truths before me daily. More specifically, I am indebted to the doctrinal teaching found recorded in the tapes of R. B. Thieme, Jr. of Houston, Texas, who is one of the leading Greek and Hebrew scholars of our time. The general emphasis of the doctrine presented in this book is very effectively outlined in the eight volumes of *Systematic Theology* written by Lewis Sperry Chafer and printed by the Dallas Seminary Press of Dallas, Texas. My personal thanks is also extended to my former secretary, Mrs. Verna Williams, for typing the manuscript.

The Pastor's Study
Immanuel Baptist Church
1000 Bishop
Little Rock, Arkansas

I

WHO IS GOD?

Knowing God is life's most significant achievement, and coming to know Him is the most exciting pilgrimage in life. There is something innate and inborn in man that tells him there is a God. The Apostle Paul referred to this concept when he wrote the first chapter of Romans. "For the invisible things of him from the creation of the world are clearly seen, being understood by the things that are made, even his eternal power and Godhead; so that they are without excuse" (Romans 1:20).

God is anxious and willing to reveal himself to man, and he has printed the reality of his being in the physical world which surrounds us. The beauty of nature, the majesty of the sky and the sea, the symmetry and design in plant and animal life all speak to us of a supreme being. And this same God has commanded man to love him, as is stated in Deuteronomy 6:5. "And thou shalt love the Lord thy God with all thy heart [mind], and with all thy soul, and with all thy might." However, a difficulty immediately arises at this point. God is invisible and cannot be seen. The Apostle John presents this idea in the opening page of his gospel when he says, "No man hath seen God at any time; the only begotten Son, who is in the bosom of the Father, he hath declared him." Therefore, we are commanded to know and to love someone we have not seen. John himself asked the very question we have raised in 1 John 4:20b: "How can he love God whom he hath not seen?" However there is an answer to this fundamental question, and that answer is The Word of God. **No man can ever know God apart from a knowledge of The Word of God.** God's character, God's essence, is clearly revealed in scripture.

If someone were to ask you, "Who is God?", what would you say? God, knowing that we would not be able to develop an accurate answer to this question from our own resources has answered it adequately and conclusively in his own Word. The question is not "What do I think God is?", but rather, "What does God's Word say that he is?". I believe the most rewarding lesson I have ever learned is the Bible's answer to this question.

God has ten characteristics, ten essence qualities. Christ has these same ten characteristics, and the Holy Spirit exhibits them as well. I find these essence qualities of God on almost every page of the Bible. I have discovered that I cannot read five verses of scripture, either in the Old or the New Testaments, without encountering one of these essence qualities.

1. GOD IS SOVEREIGN

This means that God has always existed and is the supreme ruler of the

1

universe. When Adam and Eve exhibited their negative volition and sinned by eating the forbidden fruit, God allowed Satan to move in and become the temporary ruler of the world. But this rulership of Satan is only temporary and is under the permissive will of God. God has never ceased to be the sovereign ruler of the universe, and he never will.

The psalmist expressed this idea in Psalm 46:10: "Be still, and know that I am God: I will be exalted among the heathen, I will be exalted in the earth." We find the same idea also in Psalm 97:1: "The Lord reigneth; let the earth rejoice; let the multitude of the isles be glad thereof." Paul reminds us that God will be the sovereign God forever when he says in 1 Corinthians 15:25, "For he must reign, till he hath put all enemies under his feet." Therefore, when I put my life in his hands through faith in Christ, I know that a sovereign God is able to keep me forever.

2. GOD IS ABSOLUTE RIGHTEOUSNESS

This means that everything that God does is right and that he could not do anything wrong, even if he wanted to. God is absolutely good and every decision and action of God is perfect. God has never made a mistake, and he never will. Therefore, the one who knows God will never think of making a remark like, "Why did God do that to me?". God knows you better than you know yourself and everything he ever does to you or for you is perfect and right. In Genesis 18:25 a question is raised and the construction of the Hebrew language is such that a positive answer is demanded. The question is, "Shall not the judge of all the earth do right?" And the answer is, "Certainly, the judge of all the earth will do right." Psalm 111:3 says, "His work is honourable and glorious: and his righteousness endureth forever." In Jeremiah 23:6 he is called righteousness. "In his days Judah shall be saved, and Israel shall dwell safely: and this is his name whereby he shall be called, THE LORD OUR RIGHTEOUSNESS."

3. GOD IS ABSOLUTE JUSTICE

This means that God is just and fair in all his dealings with every member of the human race. God has never been unfair and can't be unfair. He sits above time and he sees the end from the beginning. From his vantage point of perfection he knows how to act justly at all times. Matthew 5:45 says, "That ye may be the children of your Father which is in heaven: for he maketh his sun to rise on the evil and on the good, and sendeth rain on the just and on the unjust." 1 Peter 1:17 says, "And if ye call on the Father, who without respect of persons judgeth according to every man's work, pass the time of your sojourning here in fear." When injustice comes to us, it has to come from some other source than from God. God is perfectly fair, and he always has been and always will be.

4. GOD IS LOVE

This is the first verse of scripture many children learn. God's love is perfect, unchanging, absolute. We love from a limited perspective, but God loves from limitless understanding and wisdom. When we love we expect something in return, but God loves us apart from any love we ever give in return. Later on in another chapter we will discuss the difference between the **agape** (mental attitude) love of God and the **phileo** (warm, personal) love of God. But in either case, God's love is unchanging, perfect, absolute. One cannot say this too often. The greatest expression of God's love is the cross, and it includes every person of the human race. No man can ever go so far that he can stand outside the power of God's love. In Romans 5:5 Paul says, "And hope maketh not ashamed; because the love of God is shed abroad in our hearts by the Holy Ghost which is given unto us."

5. GOD IS ETERNAL LIFE

There never was a time when God did not exist. There is a difference between everlasting life and eternal life. We have everlasting life once we have believed in Christ. This means we had a beginning, but we will have no ending. But God never had any beginning and will have no ending, and we call this eternal life. The Bible uses language about God that refers to his eternity. Such words as forever and ever, everlasting, eternal, unending, refer to this dimension of his nature.

In Psalm 111:3 we read, "His work is honourable and glorious: and his righteousness endureth forever." Isaiah 9:6 says, "For unto us a child is born, unto us a son is given: and the government shall be upon his shoulder: and his name shall be called Wonderful Counsellor, The mighty God, the everlasting Father, The Prince of Peace." Why does it say a child is born and a son is given? The reason is this: Millions of years ago in eternity past God gave his Son to go to the cross to die for our sins; then in time, and at exactly the right time, that child was born.

6. GOD IS OMNISCIENT

Omniscience means that God knows all things. He knew a million years ago that I would write this book, and he knew you would be reading it, just as you are at this very moment. God has always known everything, and there never was a time when he didn't know everything. I was conducting a class with some college students and one student asked, "Do you think God understands radar?" The class broke out in laughter. Naturally they did, for they realized how foolish the question was. God knew the principles that have produced radio and television and every other invention that has just been known to us rather recently. The past, present and future are equally known to God. We are limited by time, but God sits above time.

Job understood this when he said, "I know that thou canst do every

3

thing, and that no thought can be withholden from thee." Job 42:2. Paul, in Romans 8:27, suggests that God reads our minds at all times in these words: "And he that searcheth the hearts knoweth what is in the mind of the Spirit, because he maketh intercession for the saints according to the will of God." Hebrews 4:13 says, "Neither is there any creature that is not manifest in his sight: but all things are naked and open unto the eyes of him with whom we have to do."

7. GOD IS OMNIPOTENT

All power is innate in God, and there is no limitation to the power of God. Genesis 18:14 says, "Is there anything too hard for the Lord? [The Hebrew is so constructed it means to imply, "Of course not, nothing is too hard for the Lord."] At the time appointed I will return unto thee, according to the time of life, and Sarah shall have a son." Isaish 26:4 says, "Trust ye in the Lord forever, for in the Lord Jehovah there is everlasting strength." God has the power to save and he has the power to keep us saved.

8. GOD IS OMNIPRESENT

God is everywhere. God has always been everywhere. No man can ever escape from the presence of God. Psalm 139:7-10 may be the best passage in the Bible to speak to us of the omnipresence of God: "Whither shall I go from thy spirit? or whither shall I flee from thy presence? If I ascend up into heaven, thou art there: if I make my bed in hell, behold, thou art there. If I take the wings of the morning, and dwell in the uttermost parts of the sea; even there shall thy hands lead me, and thy right hand shall hold me." Jeremiah 23:24 also says, "Can any hide himself in secret places that I shall not see him? saith the Lord. Do not I fill heaven and earth? saith the Lord."

9. GOD IS IMMUTABLE

This means that God never changes. We change, but he never changes. We become discouraged and desire to quit, but God moves on with perfect love and grace. This is why the Bible so often says, "God is faithful." Hebrews 13:8 says, "Jesus Christ, the same yesterday, and today, and forever." And Micah 3:6 says, "For I am the Lord, I change not; therefore ye sons of Jacob are not consumed."

10. GOD IS VERACITY

Everything that God has ever said is perfect truth. Jesus said that he was the way and the truth and the life. He meant that he was perfect truth and there is no error at all in God. Numbers 23:19 says, "God is not a man, that he should lie; neither the son of man, that he should repent: hath he said, and shall he not do it? or hath he spoken, and shall he not make it good?" Psalm 100:5 says, "For the Lord is good; his mercy is everlasting; and his truth endureth to all generations."

Let me ask you to run your mind quickly over these characteristics of

4

God. There they stand like jewels in a golden crown. God is SOVEREIGN — RIGHTEOUS — JUST — LOVE — ETERNAL LIFE — OMNISCIENT — OMNIPOTENT — OMNIPRESENT — IMMUTABLE — VERACITY. Every time you study scripture these characteristics of God will jump from the page into your mind. When you think of God you will think of his essence. No man can bathe his soul with these essence qualities without growing in love and appreciation for God and what God is.

Over in Deuteronomy 6:4 we read, "Hear, O Israel: The Lord our God is one Lord." Many made the serious mistake of concluding that this meant God the Father is one, and that this was written to the exclusion of Jesus Christ and the Holy Spirit. Nothing could be further from the truth. THIS VERSE MEANS THAT GOD IS ONE IN ESSENCE, BUT THREE IN PERSONALITY, as the Hebrew plural (Elohim) of the word God suggests. "ONE GOD" means that God the Father, God the Son, and God the Holy Spirit all three have exactly the same essence characteristics. It is my fervent hope that you will learn the essence of God so thoroughly that if someone were to awaken you at midnight and ask you, "Who is God?", you would be able to give these characteristics without missing a beat.

God is...

In my office where I study there is on display at all times the ten characteristics of God. I never let a day pass that I do not see them and repeat them in my mind. I wish every Sunday School class in the world could have these characteristics displayed so all could see them every Sunday. This is the beginning of our quest in the Christian walk. Again and again in this book we will be referring to the essence of God and immediately you will have this image in your mind.

Sovereignty
Righteousness
Justice
Love
Eternal Life
Omniscience
Omnipotence
Omnipresence
Immutability
Veracity

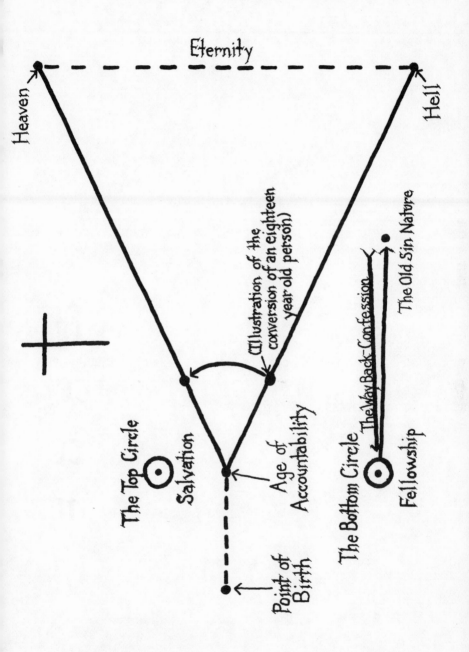

Eternity

Heaven

Hell

(Illustration of the conversion of an eighteen year old person)

The Old Sin Nature

The Way Back—Confession

The Top Circle
Salvation

Age of Accountability

The Bottom Circle
Fellowship

Point of Birth

7

SALVATION MADE PLAIN

The key in understanding the teaching of these next few pages lies in a careful examination of the chart which appears on the pages at the beginning of this chapter. For many years I have tried to witness accurately to unbelievers, and as I quoted scripture, which they were often not prepared to understand, I frequently found myself confused and bewildered. I would do my best to lead them to Christ, but too often my efforts ended in futility. I came away with the feeling I had tried to force upon the listener something he did not understand. I realized I was pushing for a decision, when instead, I should have been giving information that makes the salvation of the soul clear and understandable.

About ten years ago I began to use this chart in order to teach the truth involved in salvation. I discovered that my unsaved friend soon realized I was not attempting to force him into a decision he did not understand, but rather, I was attempting to give him information he could use in making a decision without even the suggestion of coercion from me. I found as I drew the diagram and talked about faith in Christ, my unsaved friend relaxed and began to listen intently to what was being taught. I have drawn this diagram hundreds of times, explaining each step as I moved along. I have yet to have a single person fail to say to me when the diagram was finished, "Will you please give that drawing to me?"

Please notice there is no pressure involved in a presentation of this kind. There is no attempt to get an immediate decision. The whole emphasis is on giving information which makes the issues in salvation perfectly clear.

The Starting Point

Look at the chart again carefully. We begin with the point of birth. Every person is interested in the date of his birth and this is the natural point to begin. We move out in a line until we come to the point which I choose to call "The Age of Responsibility." You may wish to call it "The Age of Accountability." This is the point where the person is old enough to think for himself and to make decisions for himself, and this is also the point where the child is old enough to distinguish right from wrong.

Death Before Accountability

Just suppose a baby or a young child dies before reaching the age of responsibility; what happens then? The Bible is quite clear in teaching that God, in his grace and mercy, takes this one to heaven and that this little one will be secure with him for eternity. This little one is saved by the grace of God.

In 2 Samuel 12:22-23 we read these lines: "And he said, While the child was yet alive, I fasted and wept: for I said, Who can tell whether God will be gracious to me, that the child may live? But now he is dead, wherefore shall I fast? can I bring him back again? I shall go to him, but he shall not return to me." The sin of David with Bathsheba resulted in the birth of this child. But 2 Samuel 12:14 says, "The child also that is born unto thee shall surely die." The child died as a part of the punishment that came to David for his sin, but God did not punish the innocent baby for the sin of the father. That is why we know God in his mercy and grace picked up that little baby and took it to heaven. This explains why David wrote, "I shall go to him but he shall not return to me."

To follow that thinking one step further, what about the person who is an idiot or imbecile and never can think for himself or make decisions for himself? God in his mercy takes him to heaven and he will spend eternity with God and all the redeemed of all the ages.

However, when a person arrives at the age of responsibility and is a normal human being, he will either believe in Christ and go the upper road and spend eternity in heaven; or he will travel the lower road of unbelief and spend eternity in hell. There is no middle ground. Every person is either saved or lost. Every person will spend eternity either in heaven or in hell.

The Story Of The Cross

This is the point in our study of this diagram where the cross comes into the picture. You will notice in the diagram the illustration of an 18-year-old young man. He has not gone very far down the road of unbelief, but unless he becomes a believer through faith in Christ he will continue the downward road that eventually leads to hell.

At this point, an explanation of Christ's atoning death on the cross is given. As I point to the cross, I remind my unsaved friend that on that cross Christ paid for every sin of the whole human race. On the cross he drank from a cup and in that cup was every sin of every man; past, present and future. I will never forget when I used this diagram for the first time with an 18-year-old man. He said with earnestness, "I want to believe in him right now. I do believe in him." I took my pencil and drew the line spanning the gulf between the lower and upper road and I said, "Then you are saved right now." I shall never forget how he looked up and smiled, "I know I am." I explained to him how he could not go back and become younger and go back to a point prior to the age of responsibility. Nevertheless, the moment he believed he jumped over this expanse that separated him from God and was saved instantly.

The Top Circle

Please notice the top circle in this diagram. The moment one believes in

10

Christ he is on the upper road to heaven and Christ puts him in the top circle, and he will never get out of that top circle for the rest of his life. The scripture says that the moment he placed his faith in Christ he was sealed by the Holy Spirit, and that seal can never be broken by Satan or by sin or by anyone or anything else.

This doctrine is taught in such scriptures as 2 Corinthians 1:22. "Who hath also sealed us, and given the earnest of the Spirit in our hearts." John 6:27: "Labour not for the meat which perisheth, but for that meat which endureth unto everlasting life, which the Son of man shall give unto you: for him hath God the Father sealed." Ephesians 1:13: "In whom ye also trusted, after that ye heard the word of truth, the gospel of your salvation: in whom also after that ye believed, ye were sealed with that holy Spirit of promise."

We will discuss the power of this seal in more detail when we come to the chapter on eternal security.

The Lower Circle

While the upper circle represents salvation and security, the lower circle represents fellowship. The moment one believes he is in the lower circle of fellowship, but unlike the top circle, if he sins he can get out. The believer still retains his old sin nature after salvation and under the influence of it, he sins and immediately is out of the bottom circle and is under the influence of Satan. Under the influence of his old sin nature he will commit any sin that he might have committed if he were still traveling the lower road. What then is he to do?

The Road Back

Since our new convert is now a believer, he can confess his sins and get back in fellowship with God. John says in 1 John 1:9, "If we [believers] confess our sins, he is faithful and just to forgive us our sins, and to cleanse us from all unrighteousness." The word for confess is **homo logeo. Homo** means "the same" and **logeo** means "to speak." Therefore, confess means simply to speak the same thing you did, to recognize your sin, to acknowledge your sin. Please notice that confession doesn't mean to feel sorry for your sin, to cry over it, or to try to make it up to God, but simply to call the sin by name.

Why Will God Forgive?

1 John 1:9 says that if we confess, acknowledge, recognize the sin God will forgive it. Why? The reason is simple. On that cross Christ paid for that sin in full. Since it has been paid for and since we have acknowledged it, all God can do is forgive us, and he does. But God does more. God is a God of grace and he always does more. We confess the sins we know about and God forgives us. But what about the sins we don't know about? 1 John 1:9 says, "and cleanse us from all unrighteousness." This final clause covers the sins

11

we don't even know about and therefore can't confess them. Thus, the verse taken as a whole, points the way beyond those sins we know about and we confess and even those that remain beyond our explicit recognition.

A Personal Note

I would like to add my personal feeling about 1John 1:9. I believe for daily Christian living it is the most important verse in the Bible. It is the first verse I flee to each morning as I face God. I quickly take an inventory of the day before and attempt to confess every sin of my mind and hand and tongue. In less than a second I know I am back in the bottom circle of Fellowship with him and that's where I attempt to stay. The more mature a believer becomes, the more time he spends in the bottom circle and the less time he spends out under the influence of the old sin nature.

Sin And Sins

Please notice in this diagram the truth has been clearly portrayed that the believer can deal with only **one** sin before his salvation and that one sin is the sin of unbelief. After his salvation he can deal with **sins** (plural), and this he does by means of confession with the power of Christ and the Holy Spirit within him.

Before I understood John 16:8 I thought the issue in the eye of the unbeliever was sins. "And when he is come, he will reprove the world of sin, and of righteousness, and of judgment." However, this verse taught me that the Holy Spirit only convicts the unbeliever of one sin, and that sin is failing to believe in Christ. This is clearly stated in John 16:9. "Of sin, because they believe not on me." This is the cardinal sin, and if a man goes to hell it is because of this sin and his failure to believe in Christ. Therefore, in witnessing we must never make sins the issue but center on Christ and faith in him.

Look At These Principles

In this diagram we have presented many of the great doctrinal truths involved in salvation.
1. Man is a sinner at birth, not because of anything he has done, but because he is born with an old sin nature.
2. Man is safe until he comes to the age of responsibility, and if he dies before that time, God in his grace takes him to heaven.
3. The moment one believes in Christ he is on the upper road to heaven. He is sealed in the top circle by the Holy Spirit, and he is eternally secure.
4. If one does not believe in Christ, he continues on the lower road that leads to hell.
5. The bottom circle is the circle of fellowship. While the believer is in that circle he is filled with the Holy Spirit, and as long as he stays there he will not sin. Once he yields to a temptation from Satan, or from the pull of his old sin nature, he is out of the bottom circle and is out of fellowship.

An Explanation Of The Old Sin Nature

What is this thing we call the Old Sin Nature and where did it come from? Again, we will use a diagram to explain this important truth. When God placed Adam and Eve in the Garden of Eden they were what we call Trichotomous. They were body, soul and spirit. The moment they ate of the forbidden fruit, they blacked out their human spirit and got an Old Sin Nature.

First, the woman ate of the fruit and became a sinner. Then Adam ate and received his Old Sin Nature. However, there was a difference in the result of their acts. The woman was deceived by Satan and didn't understand what she had done. Adam, with full understanding, ate deliberately. Therefore, God held Adam responsible for sin and the Old Sin Nature comes down through the seed of the man, not through the seed of the woman. They both became sinners when they ate of the forbidden fruit, but God held Adam responsible.

This is clearly explained by Paul in 1 Timothy 2:13-14. Both sinned and both received an Old Sin Nature, but Adam was held responsible because he understood the implication of his act. This is why Paul wrote in 1 Cor. 15:22, "For as in Adam all die, even so in Christ shall all be made alive." Adam, the federal head of the human race, was held responsible for sin. The Old Sin Nature comes down through the seed of the man, not through the seed of the woman.

The Importance Of The Virgin Birth

Every man gets his Old Sin Nature from his father, not from his mother. Every woman gets her Old Sin Nature from her father, not from her mother. Therefore, if a man could be born of a woman without a father, he would not have an Old Sin Nature. Jesus was born of Mary without a human father and, therefore, he did not have an Old Sin Nature. During his thirty-three years on earth he never committed an act of sin, and that is why Paul could write in 2 Cor. 5:21, "For he hath made him to be sin for us, who knew no sin [never had an Old Sin Nature and never committed an act of sin]; that we might be made the righteousness of God in him."

The Fig Leaves And The Coats Of Skin

Once Adam and Eve had eaten of the forbidden fruit they were sinners. This is why they hid themselves when Christ came into the Garden looking for them. (You notice I say "Christ" came looking for them. This is correct and I will explain this more in detail later on. All through these verses in Genesis we read the words "The Lord God" and this double term contains a reference to the Christ. Christ is always the manifest one in the Godhead.)

In Genesis 3:9 we read the words, "And the Lord God called unto Adam, and said unto him, 'Where art thou?'" A more correct translation of

13

that Hebrew is "Adam, why are you where you are?"

Once Adam and Eve had admitted their guilt, Christ explained to them that fig leaf aprons (the creation of their hands) would not cover their sin. He explained to them what he would one day do to pay for their sins on the cross, and if they would believe on him he would make coats of skin and clothe them.

At the first tree they said, "I will disobey," and they became sinners. Now, at the second tree they said, "I will believe," and Christ made coats of skin and clothed them. Thus Adam and Eve became the first two Christians of the human race.

> [NOTE: In Genesis 3:21 we read "Unto Adam also and to his wife did the Lord God (which is Jesus Christ) make coats of skins and clothed them."]

We have to read what we know of the essence of God into this incident to understand what happened here. God is perfect justice and he has never forced the human will of any man since the beginning of the human race. Adam and Eve understood this issue and freely accepted Christ's provision for them. This is the first recorded act of faith in scripture and is a picture of the salvation of every believer since that time.

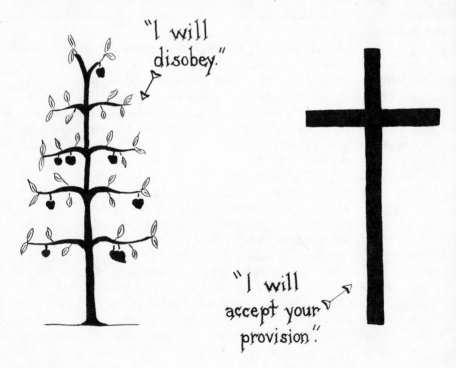

Salvation Pictured In Baptism By Immersion

Look at the salvation diagram again. See how the unbeliever put his faith in Christ and went from the lower road of condemnation to the upper road of salvation and eternal life. This is precisely what is pictured in baptism by immersion. I place the new convert under the water, and under the water he cannot breathe. If he were to stay there he would die. This is a picture of his life before he believed in Christ. He was dead in his trespasses and sins. In the next moment, I bring him up out of the water where he can breathe again, and this is a picture of life, his new-found life in Christ. Baptism by immersion pictures the salvation of the new believer. Even a little child can understand this great truth, and before I baptize anyone I go over this truth very carefully. Thus, baptism becomes a very sacred experience and becomes a tool for teaching doctrinal truth.

III

BELIEVE, PLUS NOTHING!

For a good many years I have had the conviction that the most mis-understood doctrine of Christianity is the doctrine of salvation. What does a man have to do in order to be saved? The answer most often given goes something like this: "Repent of your sins and believe in Christ." This answer is given with the idea that if the unsaved person will be sorry for his sins, turn from his sins, turn over a new leaf (some even say, "You have been walking in one direction, now turn and walk in the opposite direction"), then if you will believe in Christ, you will be saved. In some ways the total doctrinal emphasis of this book is to challenge that idea and to demonstrate from scripture that the unbeliever must only do one thing to be saved, and that one thing is to believe in Jesus Christ.

The Bible's Clearest Statement Of Salvation

The clearest statement in all the Word of God of the plan of salvation is found in Acts 16:31 when Paul and Silas said to the Philippian jailer, "Believe on the Lord Jesus Christ and thou shalt be saved." This is precisely what every man must do to be saved and no matter how many other things we attempt to attach to salvation, faith in Jesus Christ is the only thing necessary.

This very same emphasis is given in Genesis 15:6 where the conversion of Abraham is recorded. This verse says, "And he believed in the Lord: and he counted it to him for righteousness." A little more accurate reading of the Hebrew says, "And he had believed [possibly as much as 40 or 50 years earlier] in the Lord; and he [God the Father] counted it to him for righteous-ness." Here is belief plus nothing. However, man is of such nature that he makes himself believe he has to do something, he has to make changes in his life, he has to feel sorry for his sins, he has to change the direction of his life, and only if he will do all these things can he turn to Christ and be saved.

The True Meaning Of Repentance

In the Greek New Testament we have two words that are translated "Repent." One is **meta noeo** and it means to "change your thinking" or "change your mind." The other word is **meta mellomai** and it, too, is translated "Repent" but it simply means to be sorry for something, to have an emotional regret, but it does not imply repentance, such as a change of mind or will. As an illustration of **meta mellomai,** we read in Matthew 27:3, "Then Judas, which had betrayed him, when he saw that he was condemned, repented himself..." Now that word, "repented himself," means Judas was sorry for his act of betrayal, but he never changed his mind about Christ, he

17

never believed in Christ and he died unsaved and will spend eternity in hell.

Repentance For The Unsaved Man

For the unsaved man, repent and believe are heads and tails of the same coin. They go together. You cannot repent without believing and you cannot believe without repenting. Repent is negative and believe is positive and they are halves of the same whole. Repentance, for the unsaved man, is beamed toward Christ, never toward sin. Repentance, for the unsaved man, means to change his mind about Christ. At one moment a man does not believe, then he repents, he changes his mind about Christ, believes and is saved. Therefore, repentance for the unsaved is a change of mental attitude concerning Christ.

No unsaved man can repent of his sins. If he could repent of one sin, then he could repent of all of his sins, and if he could do this there would be no reason for him to go to the cross and be saved. On the cross Christ paid for every sin of every man of the whole human race. He paid for those sins in toto. When we sing "Jesus Paid It All," we are singing correct doctrine, for in the atonement Jesus Christ satisfied the righteousness and the justice of God and the total debt for sins was paid in full. If Christ handled all our sins on the cross, and he did, we can do nothing concerning our sins, for Christ has already done it all. Therefore, repentance for the unsaved man is beamed toward Christ, not toward sins. A man changes his mind about Christ, and in a second of time, when he beams positive volition toward Christ, he is born again.

When a man is unsaved he can deal with only one sin, and that is the sin of unbelief. In fact, the unsaved man can pray only one prayer and that prayer is: "God, be merciful to me, a sinner." Therefore, when we go out to win men to Christ, we should never mention sins. We should only mention Christ. For the unsaved man, sins are not the issue; Christ is the issue.

This doctrine of dealing with only one sin, the sin of unbelief, is beautifully explained in John 16:8-9. This passage says, "When he is come [referring to God the Holy Spirit] he will reprove the world of sin, and of righteousness, and of judgment: of sin, because they believe not on me." Please notice that these verses say that the Holy Spirit will reprove [the word is **alegcho** and it means lay it on the line, make it perfectly clear] the world of sin.... The word for sin is **hamartia** in the singular. The only sin of which the Holy Spirit convicts the unsaved man is the sin of unbelief. Sins (plural) will be dealt with after the man becomes a Christian. The issue of salvation concerns one sin and one sin only, and that is the sin of unbelief. Therefore, sins are not the issue in salvation. Sin, the sin of unbelief, is the issue. After one becomes a believer, then Christ moves in and the Holy Spirit moves in and at that time sins become the issue. Countless millions have been driven

18

away from Christianity because so-called sincere and devoted soul-winners have gone out to witness and have made sins the issue rather than sin. I repeat: The Holy Spirit only deals with one sin in the life of the unbeliever and that sin is failure to believe in Christ.

It may be that by this time you think that this approach ignores the awfulness and reality of sins. Just the opposite is the truth. Sins are real, and the old sin nature will continue to dog the steps of the believer every day of his Christian life. However, once a person puts his faith in Christ he then has a power from within himself to confront sins. Christ is within and the Holy Spirit is within, and they become a mighty force to help combat sins day by day.

Therefore, we conclude, one sin is dealt with before salvation, and that sin is unbelief in Christ. Once that sin is removed by faith in Christ, the new believer is now ready to begin his daily battle against sins. The unsaved man repents of one sin, the sin of unbelief, by changing his mind about Christ. Once he has experienced salvation, he repents of sins every day, and this he does by confession according to 1 John 1:9.

Confession For The Saved Man

Once a man has believed in Christ and is saved, he then discovers he still has an old sin nature and is tempted to sin every day, possibly many times a day. When he sins he discovers he is out of fellowship and is under the control of his old sin nature. Now he can repent of sins and this he does by confessing these sins. 1 John 1:9 says, "If we confess our sins he is faithful and just to forgive us our sins, and to cleanse us of all unrighteousness." As I have indicated already, the word confess is from **homo logeo** which means to name your sin, recognize your sins, acknowledge your sins. It does not mean feel sorry for sins or cry over your sins or say, "I'll never do it again," The reason why your sins are forgiven when you confess them is explained by what Christ did on the cross. While he was on that cross, he drank from a cup, and in that cup were all the sins of every man of all time. He drank those sins down, so to speak, paid for them, crushed them. When you confess a sin God looks at the cross and says to the sinner, "My son paid for those sins on the cross, and since you have acknowledged them, all I can do is forgive them and I do forgive them." This is the explanation of how one sin, the sin of unbelief, is dealt with before salvation, and sins (plural) are dealt with after salvation.

Believe, Plus Nothing

You will notice that the title of this chapter is the same as the title of the book. Can it really be true that a man is saved by faith in Christ and faith alone? One of the most misunderstood passages in the Bible is the often quoted verses of Romans 10:8-10. "But what saith it? The word is nigh unto thee, even in thy mouth, and in thy heart: that is, the word of faith, which we preach; that if thou shalt confess with thy mouth the Lord Jesus, and shalt believe in thine heart that God hath raised him from the dead, thou shalt be saved. For with the heart man believeth unto righteousness; and with the mouth confession is made unto salvation."

I ask you to read these three verses very carefully. In the heart of this passage we find the words, "That if thou shalt believe in thy heart that God hath raised him from the dead, thou shalt be saved." At first reading, this passage seems to say that one must confess Jesus Christ with his lips in order to be saved. If this passage really does say this, then we might go on to say that he must also repent of his sins, he must raise his hand, he must walk down an aisle, he must sign a card, he must join a church, and then must be baptized; then, if he will do all these things, he will be saved.

The Real Emphasis Of This Passage

The real emphasis of Romans 10:8-10 is not the plan of salvation, but is, rather, Paul's explanation to the Jewish people of the reason for their failure to witness about Christ to the world. God intended for the Jewish people to accept Christ and to witness to all the people in the world concerning Christ. But instead they became enamored with the law of Moses and the Ten Commandments and Jewish ritual. In so doing, they walked past the cross and never mentioned Christ's atoning death on the cross. Paul wrote this passage to explain this Jewish failure.

Verse 8: "But what sayeth it? The word is nigh thee, even in thy mouth and in thy heart: that is, the word of faith, which we preach." This "it" in the first phrase is very important. This "it" refers to salvation, to faith in Christ. So this verse says, "What does faith in Christ say?"

Paul next uses a regular custom of the Greeks and that custom was to speak in reverse order. He is going to mention the lesser things first, and then the more important thing last. You recall Jesus did this often. In John 14:6 Jesus said, "I am the way, the truth and the life..." Now, which is more important; the way, the truth or the life? The life is most important for everything else depends upon it. But once you have Life, then out from Life comes Truth. Once you know the truth, then you know the way you are to go. So Jesus spoke in reverse order when he referred to the way, the truth and the life. The Apostle Paul did precisely the same thing in Romans 10:8 when he said, "The word is nigh thee, even in thy mouth and in thy heart." (Please understand that when the Bible uses the word heart it is referring to the mind, the place where we do our thinking and where the soul and spirit reside.)

Now, let me ask you a question. Where are your words? Are they first in your mouth and then in your mind? Well, I hope not. Paul was speaking in

20

reverse. You form your words in your mind and then you speak them in your mouth, or this is certainly the way it should be. Once you form the words in your mind, then you speak them with your lips. The point Paul was making to the Jews was this, "You failed to accept Christ in your mind; therefore, you did not confess (witness about him) with your lips." Their failure was a failure to accept Christ; therefore, they didn't confess him to others.

Look at Verse 9. "That if thou shalt confess with thy mouth the Lord Jesus, and shalt believe in thy heart God hath raised him from the dead, thou shalt be saved." The first word, "that," is from **hoti** and introduces a result clause. Confessing Christ with the lips is a result of believing on Christ in the mind; therefore, confessing Christ with the lips is not a means to salvation, but is a result of salvation. Paul is still using that same reverse order in this verse. Believing on Jesus Christ in the mind comes first, and as a result, there is witnessing with the lips.

Please notice this verse says, "Confess with thy mouth that Jesus is Lord." The Romans all said, "Caesar is Lord." Paul was reminding them that they were to go out and witness to the fact that "Jesus is Lord." Paul again in this verse is referring to Jewish failure. They failed to believe in their minds, and as a result they didn't witness with their lips. Paul then includes the words, "That God hath raised him from the dead." Does a man have to believe that God raised him from the dead in order to be saved? No, he does not. The Jews, however, were very weak on the resurrection and Paul inserted this phrase at this point to give emphasis to belief in the resurrection, which also is a result of salvation, not a means to salvation.

An informed believer will believe in the resurrection because it is a vital part of the gospel and illustrates who Jesus is. Jesus is God, and you can't keep God in a grave. His resurrection from the dead declared to the world who he was and Paul included these words to remind the Jews that they had played down the resurrection. Belief in the resurrection comes as a result of knowing who Christ really is. He is God and the grave did not end his life or his work. His resurrection let the world know who he was.

Romans 10:10. "For with the heart man believeth unto righteousness: and with the mouth confession is made unto salvation." In this verse Paul gives the proper sequence. It is as if Paul were saying something like this: "Don't get confused; don't get the cart before the horse. Keep the sequence clear." Therefore he says, "For with the heart man believeth unto righteousness [salvation]." This is the plan of salvation, clearly stated. Then Paul adds, "And with the mouth confession is made unto salvation." The Greek text says, "And with the mouth confession is made as a result of salvation." Witnessing is always the result of salvation and never a means to salvation.

Verse 11. "For the scripture saith, whosoever believeth on him shall not

21

be ashamed." This is a quotation of Isaiah 28:16. It means that whosoever believeth in Christ will never stand at the judgment, will never be ashamed. Therefore, this passage is not a passage on the plan of salvation, but rather a passage in which Paul explains to the Jews the real reason for their failure. Having failed to believe in Christ in their hearts (minds), they naturally failed to witness to the world about Christ. Witnessing is always the result of salvation.

Summary

Let us summarize what has been said in this great passage, Romans 10:8-10.

1. This is a passage explaining the failure of the Jews. Since they failed to believe in Christ, naturally they failed to witness.
2. The unsaved man can repent of only one sin, and that is the sin of unbelief. After salvation, the saved man repents of sins by means of confession. 1 John 1:9.
3. The Holy Spirit convicts the unsaved man at only one point, the point of unbelief. The Holy Spirit deals with only one sin (hamartia) before salvation. After salvation Christ and the Holy Spirit work from within the life to combat sins.
4. Man can do nothing in order to be saved, since Christ has already accomplished all the work for salvation on the cross. "Believe" is a non-meritorious verb. All the credit is in the object, not the subject.
5. If the unsaved man could repent of one sin, then he could repent of all sins, and this would eliminate the need for the cross. The only thing a sinner can do to be saved is to believe in Christ, change his mind about Christ. Therefore, sin is not the issue in salvation; Christ is the issue.
6. Man is proud by nature and it is very difficult for him to admit that he can do nothing to aid in his salvation. But salvation by grace through faith means that Christ does it all and that man can only accept "the all" from Christ.

Therefore, the title of this book and this chapter is scripturally correct —

BELIEVE, PLUS NOTHING.

22

In some of our songbooks there is a very beautiful song written by E. M. Bartlett of Arkansas. It is a very lovely song because it reminds us of the victory Jesus brings into the life of the believer. However, the theology of the first verse in the song is inaccurate. Let me quote the words.

"I heard an old, old story,
  How a Saviour came from glory,
  How he gave his life on Calvary
  To save a wretch like me:
  I heard about his groaning,
  Of his precious blood's atoning,
  Then I repented of my sins and won the victory."*

I think I understand what the writer was trying to say, but the theology is incorrect. At my salvation I did not do something that won the victory. The truth is that Christ did something that won the victory and that something was his atoning work on the cross. I did absolutely nothing to win the victory. After Christ had paid for my every sin he exclaimed **tetelestai** meaning "It is finished." (This is the perfect tense of the verb **teleo** meaning to complete, to end, to finish.) The whole victory over sin was won that day and the work was finished forever — we did not win the victory, Jesus won the victory; and by faith we accept his gift of salvation. It is for this reason that I believe the greatest truth included in the message of salvation is "Believe, Plus Nothing."

IV

WILL SALVATION LAST?

Men, by nature, like absolutes. They are drawn to something that is certain and abiding. This is why when we purchase something of real value we like to have a written guarantee. The greatest gift God has ever given us is eternal salvation through his own son, Jesus Christ. In these next pages I want to look carefully at the great passages in the Word of God where eternal abiding salvation is delineated clearly.

Ye Are Fallen From Grace

The words, "Ye are fallen from grace," are the last phrase of Galatians 5:4. Paul addressed these remarks to Galatian believers. He, earlier in the chapter, had warned the Christians in Galatia to stand fast in their freedom. Once they had believed in Christ they were free from the bondage of sin. Everywhere Paul went the hallmark of his preaching was salvation by grace through faith. One of the clearest statements in scripture concerning this truth is to be found in Galatians 2:15. "Knowing that a man is not justified by the works of the law, but by the faith in Jesus Christ, even we have believed in Jesus Christ, that we might be justified by the faith in Christ, and not by the works of the law: for by the works of the law shall no flesh be justified."

The Judaizers followed Paul everywhere he went and always attempted to undermine him at the point of salvation by grace through faith. They would say something like this: "Did Paul say you could be saved by faith and faith alone?" And when the audience would reply, "Yes, that's exactly what he said," the Judaizers would begin their skillful, infiltrating deception. One can almost hear them down across these intervening centuries as they would say, "Now, Paul knows better than that! You know you have to keep the law of Moses, you have to keep the Ten Commandments, you have to be circumcised before you can be saved." This is why Paul wrote such statements as Galatians 3:13: "Christ hath redeemed us from the curse of the law, being made a curse for us: for it is written, cursed is every one that hangeth on a tree."

The Bottom Circle

You have studied already the salvation diagram at the beginning of Chapter II. You remember "The Bottom Circle." The Bottom Circle is the circle of fellowship, for when a believer sins he falls out of the bottom circle and is immediately out of fellowship and is under the control of the Old Sin Nature. The only way to get back into fellowship is through confession, as clearly outlined in 1 John 1:9. "Ye are fallen from grace" is addressed to

25

believers only, and is referring to fellowship, not salvation. There is not one statement in all of scripture that even faintly suggests that a man can fall from salvation (the Top Circle in the diagram). No one ever has and no one ever will fall from salvation.

The moment a sinner believes in Jesus Christ he is eternally saved and at that moment is "in Christ." This is his position and will be his position forever. He is in Christ at the moment of his highest peaks of spiritual achievement, but also at the lowest depths of his carnality or disobedience. Once a man is in Christ, he is in Christ to stay. Romans 8:1 says, "There is therefore now no condemnation [judgment] to them that are in Christ Jesus." This is the great doctrine we call positional truth.

Paul knew there would be those who would not believe in eternal security and would lead believers astray, trying to persuade them that they could be lost after they are saved. In response, the logic of the reasoning of Paul in Romans 5 is something like this: Christ did the most for us at the cross, where he paid the price for all our sins. If he did the most for us while we were yet sinners, what will he do for us, now that we are saved? And Paul answers in Romans 5, "More than the most." This something "more" is to keep us saved once we have believed in Christ. This is the "much more" of the grace of God.

Why Men Doubt Eternal Security

Why is it that so many millions of believers all through the centuries have allowed themselves to believe that a saved person can be lost again after he has been saved? There are two main reasons that produce this erroneous thinking. One is a lack of knowledge of the scripture concerning the doctrine of salvation. The other reason is that people begin with human experience and base their belief about salvation on what they think they see in the lives of the Christians they observe.

Let us take Mr. X as an illustration. Mr. X believed in Christ, joined the church and was baptized. For quite some time he lived what appeared to be a very consecrated and happy Christian life. Later Mr. X began to give up his church loyalty, was less and less regular in church attendance, and finally dropped out completely, saying he never planned to go back again. Quite often the superficial observer will say, "See, Mr. X really wasn't genuinely saved in the first place. But if he was, then he has lost his salvation." What does the scripture say to erroneous thinking of this kind?

We Are Held In His Hand

I was converted when I was a very small boy, and I recall one of the scriptures which meant so much to me as a young Christian — John 10:28-29, "And I give unto them eternal life; and they shall never perish, neither shall any man pluck them out of my hand. My father, which gave them to me, is greater than all; and no man is able to pluck them out of my Father's hand." This passage lets us know that the security in salvation doesn't come from the human side, but rather from the divine side. If salvation were a matter of holding on, and the holding on depended on us, then who would be able to hold out to the end? But such is not the case. The security in salvation comes from God's power and from God's amazing grace. John has stated for us in these two verses the amazing omnipotence of God. He not only holds us in his hand once we put our faith in him, but he keeps us there forever. It is my absolute conviction that Christ is powerful enough to keep every person he has ever saved. God the Father also holds us in his hand, and with both Christ the Son and God the Father holding us, there is not the slightest possibility for us ever to lose our salvation.

In more than four decades as a pastor of churches, it has been my delightful privilege to talk with hundreds of boys and girls about faith in Christ. Somewhere along the way in the interview I take the hand of the boy or girl in my hand, and then I quote John's wonderful line as I remind them that Christ says he will hold on to them forever. Then as I place my other hand on top of theirs, I remind them that God the Father is holding on, too. Then I say to them: "With Christ holding on one side, and God the Father holding on the other side, there is no possibility for a believer ever to be lost, once he has trusted Christ."

In Matthew 24:13 we have these words: "But he that shall endure unto the end, the same shall be saved." It is easy to pick this verse up out of context and attempt to prove that if the believer will be faithful down to the end of his life, then he will be saved. But this verse is not a verse about salvation. This verse is a part of the great "Olivet Discourse" Jesus had with his disciples as he described to them the coming events of the tribulation and his second coming to this earth. This verse really says: "But he that shall endure until the end of the tribulation, the same shall be **delivered.**"

The word that is translated "saved" is from **sozo** and it means deliverance as well as salvation. Many places in scripture we must translate **sozo** to mean deliverance. Jesus was giving instructions to the Jews who would be in Palestine at the time of his second coming, and he was telling them how to conduct themselves under those terrifying circumstances. Therefore he said that if they would follow his careful instructions they would be delivered.

If having eternal security in salvation depended on the power of the believer, then no one would make it. But it does not depend on our ability or our power, but rather upon the power of God. This holding power in John 10:28 and 29 is in the hands of Christ and in the hands of God, not in our weak hands.

The Faithfulness Of God

Again and again we read in scripture "God is faithful" or "He abideth faithful." God is faithful all the time, and because he is immutable and never changes, his faithfulness is constant. We are different from God. Our faithfulness is not as constant as his, and because of this we go up and down. As the little poem says, "Today we are eager and brave, and tomorrow not caring to try." But this merely reflects our human frailty and doesn't affect the consistency and stability of God.

Anticipating this vacillation on our part about salvation, the Holy Spirit led Paul to write 2 Timothy 2:11-13: "It is a faithful saying: for if we be dead with him, we shall also live with him: If we suffer, we shall also reign with him: if we deny him, he also will deny us: If we believe not, yet he abideth faithful: he cannot deny himself."

Those words, "If we be dead with him," means we have been to the cross, have believed in him and actually died with him. "If we deny him, he also will deny us," means that if we are unfaithful, he will deny us certain rewards. Then when Paul says, "If we believe not," these words mean that the time might even come when we would denounce him and say that we no longer believed and we no longer wanted to be Christians. But Paul concludes, "He abideth faithful: he cannot deny himself."

Salvation Is A Family Affair

We are not children of God because we are members of the human race. We are children of God because of our faith in Jesus Christ. Paul says in Galatians 3:26, "For ye are all the children of God by faith in Jesus Christ." The scripture again and again portrays born-again people as being members of the family of God. When we are born into a human family, we are in that family forever. Once you are your father's son and your mother's son, you remain their son forever. There might come a time when you decide you wish to claim no relationship with your father and mother; however, you would still be their son. On the other hand, there might come a circumstance that would cause your parents to disown you, but you would still be their child. Once in the family, you are in the family to stay. In this connection, John 1:12 says, "But as many as received him, to them gave he power to become the sons of God, even to them that believe on his name."

Very close to this family analogy is the idea of the body of Christ. The moment we believe in Christ we become members of the body of Christ. At the moment of salvation the Holy Spirit picks up the believer and enters him into union with Christ. 1 Corinthians 12:12 says, "For as the body is one, and hath many members, and all the members of that one body, being many, are one body; so also is Christ."

Our Inheritance Will Last

The moment we believe in Christ he gives to us eternal life. Possibly I should say "everlasting life." As I have indicated already, there is a slight

28

difference between eternal life and everlasting life. God has eternal life, because he had no beginning and will have no ending. We have everlasting life, because we had a beginning, and once we believe in him we will have no ending. God gives to us an inheritance, and this inheritance is everlasting life with God with a perfect resurrection body in a heaven that is perfect and abiding.

1 Peter 1:4-5 is one of the Bible's strongest statements about eternal security. "To an inheritance incorruptible, and undefiled, and that fadeth not away, reserved in heaven for you, who are kept by the power of God through faith unto salvation ready to be revealed in the last time." The power of God to save us from sin is a power that indeed is amazing. But his power does not stop at the cross. It continues on through all of our lifetime and then on through eternity. There is a little sentence of gold in the one chapter Book of Jude, Verse 23, which constitutes a solemn pledge God has made to every believer of all time. This verse says, "Now unto him that is able to keep you from falling, and to present you faultless before the presence of his glory with exceeding joy."

The Tense Of Certain Greek Words Prove Eternal Security

In Acts 16:31 we read, "And they said, believe on the Lord Jesus Christ, and thou shalt be saved, and thy house." That word believe is in the aorist tense, the active voice, and the imperative mood. The aorist tense means that in a point of time one believes in Christ. Christ picks that point of time up and throws it clear into eternity. The active voice indicates that every individual must believe for himself and that no one can believe for another. The imperative mood means that belief is not optional. It is commanded by God to be the only way of salvation. "Be saved" carries the very same idea and means you will be saved on and on throughout eternity.

The Seal Of The Holy Spirit

Go back again to that top circle in our salvation diagram.

The moment one believes in Christ the Holy Spirit picks up that believer, puts him in the top circle, and seals him in forever. 2 Corinthians 1:22 says, "Who hath also sealed us, and given the earnest of the spirit in our hearts." There is no force in the universe strong enough to break that seal. Sin can't do it. Satan and demons can't do it. No force on earth or in heaven can invalidate the power of God's everlasting salvation.

This is explained in Hebrews 6:6. To understand Hebrews 6:6 you must go back to Hebrews 6:4 to get the whole meaning of this scripture. Hebrews 6:4 begins with the words, "It is impossible [then there is a long parenthesis for the rest of that verse and also verse 5, then the statement is picked up again] if they shall fall away, to renew them again unto repentance; seeing they crucify to themselves the Son of God afresh, and put him to an open shame."

This verse is talking about believers who fall out of fellowship, out of the bottom circle and will not confess their sins. It is impossible to renew them again to their former state of fellowship. Christ died once on the cross, and he is not going to come back to the earth and do it over again. It was a-once-and-for-all event. Men can be saved only once. But they can be renewed into the bottom circle of fellowship the moment they confess their sins as stated in 1 John 1:9.

A Short Summary Of This Amazing Doctrine

1. Salvation is the work of Christ and his work only. Man does nothing to achieve salvation. He only believes and thereby appropriates for himself the result of Christ's work on the cross.
2. The power that keeps a man saved, once he has believed, is the power of God. God's hand holds on. Christ's hand holds on. God's faithfulness prevails. Man's power is not involved in keeping himself in a saved condition.
3. God gives only one kind of salvation and it is everlasting, eternal, never ending.
4. Christ never saves a man twice, only once.
5. The Bible is filled with language that demonstrates eternal security. The Bible is always talking about everlasting life, about forever and forever, about never perishing, about the keeping power of God.
6. The Seal of the Holy Spirit around the soul of a believer has never been broken and can never be broken. Christ's great cry on the cross, "It is finished," carried with it the idea that the price for sin has been fully paid, and the results of that victory will abide forever.

V

THE FOUR WILLS OF GOD

Sooner or later every true believer is faced with the question, "What is the will of God for my life?" In another place in this book I have referred to the famous statement of the late Dr. George W. Truett — 47 years the pastor of the First Baptist Church of Dallas, Texas. He said:

"To know the will of God is the greatest knowledge;

To find the will of God is the greatest discovery;

To do the will of God is the greatest achievement."

I also stated that one cannot know the will of God apart from knowing the word of God, for within the word of God the will of God is revealed.

There is undisputed evidence in the word of God which points to the fact that God is anxious to reveal his will to us. One of the verses that served as a bright guiding light to my path during my student days was Isaiah 30:21: "And thine ears shall hear a word behind thee, saying, This is the way, walk ye in it, when ye turn to the right hand, and when ye turn to the left."

Quite often when doubts came to my mind because of the difficult financial burden I carried to remain in school through the most terrible depression our nation ever experienced, I often fled to this verse: "Fear thou not; for I am with thee: be not dismayed; for I am thy God: I will strengthen thee; yea, I will help thee; yea, I will uphold thee with the right hand of my righteousness." Isaiah 41:10.

In this discussion of the four wills of God I am going to use the life of Balaam as background material as revealed in Numbers 22 and following.

The Setting

Balaam's experience in his attempt to curse the nation of Israel and thereby gain the great financial price promised to him by Balak, King of Moab, occurred in the fortieth year of the wandering of the children of Israel in the wilderness. It occurred during their eighth encampment following the death of Aaron. As Israel was moving north to go past the Dead Sea and came to the place where they would cross the Jordan River and enter the land, they had to go across and through part of the Kingdom of Moab. King Balak, knowing how Israel had soundly defeated several other nations, was frightened beyond imagination. To offset what they might do, he decided to send for Balaam and have him pronounce a curse on Israel. This story is related in Numbers 22.

The Background Of Balaam

Balaam lived several hundreds of miles to the north of Moab at Pethor.

31

His father, Beor, had been steeped in demonism and wizardry. We might say that his family was head of the Eastern world's black magic organization. If Balaam's family had a sign over their place of business in Pethor it probably said something like this:

"We Curse People — Cities — Nations — For a Price." Numbers 27:7 tells us that King Balak sent a delegation to Pethor and offered Balaam a large reward if he would make the trip with them back to Moab and would pronounce a curse on Israel.

Balaam, A Believer

Balaam had become a believer I am sure, contrary to what you may read in a good many Bible commentaries. There are at least six reasons why I know that this was the case.

1. Balaam knew the Lord and confessed it in Numbers 22, Verses 8, 13, 19, and 38.
2. Balaam would not leave Pethor without the permission of the Lord. Numbers 22:8 and 12.
3. The Lord confronted Balaam and talked with him. Numbers 22:35.
4. The Lord put words in Balaam's mouth, words of blessing, when Balaam tried to curse Israel.
5. Balaam called Jehovah "His God" in Numbers 22:18.
6. The Holy Spirit came upon Balaam Numbers 24:2.

Add all of these reasons together and you have insurmountable evidence that Balaam was a believer, though a very weak and mixed up believer.

The Direct Will Of God

The first evidence we have that it was the direct will of God for Balaam not to go to Moab and pronounce a curse on Israel is in Numbers 22:12. "And God said unto Balaam, thou shalt not go with them; thou shalt not curse the people for they are blessed." There is no way to be mistaken about the will of God for Balaam concerning this journey. However, Balaam wanted the promised reward so desperately, we will see him keep on asking for permission to go and God will finally give him permission. What does this teach us? (It is quite clear that the definite, direct and perfect will of God was that Balaam not go to Moab to pronounce a curse on Israel.) However, not being willing to accept the direct will of God, let us notice how a second will of God moves into the picture. The elders of Moab returned to King Balak and reported that Balaam would not come with them back to Moab. Balak sent them again, with a much larger reward in their hands. This time we read something that sounds very strange in our ears. Numbers 22:20, "And God came unto Balaam at night, and said to him, if the men come to call thee, rise up and go with them; but yet the Word which I shall say unto thee, that shalt thou do." Quite clearly we can immediately know that this was not God's first and direct will for Balaam. For lack of a better term, I call it the permissive will of God. I know God didn't want him to go because of Numbers 22:22, "And God's anger was kindled because he went; and the Angel of the Lord stood in the way for an adversary against him ..."

What does all this mean? I think it is a very important point of doctrine that we should understand clearly. God knew Balaam wanted to go and wanted to win that fabulous reward Balak had promised to give him. God never violates human volition, and though God knew Balaam should not go, he permitted him to go under what I call the permissive will of God. God is too much of a gentleman to violate human volition. He never has and he never will reach his hand in and push human volition in any direction. Therefore, Balaam made that long trip from Pethor down to Moab intending to curse Israel and win his fortune from Balak.

The Overruling Will Of God

Once Balaam had arrived in Moab, King Balak took him to the mountain peaks so he could look down on the camps of Israel. It must have been a very impressive sight, the whole camp of Israel of some two million people down in the valley below. We know that God had restricted Balaam in what he would say, for we read in Numbers 22:35, "And the Angel of the Lord said unto Balaam, go with the men: but only the word that I shall speak unto thee, that thou shalt speak. So Balaam went with the princes of Balak."

A Blessing Instead Of A Cursing

Therefore, we see Balaam was at last in Moab, under the permissive will of God. Balak led him to the mountaintop and stood there waiting for Balaam to pronounce a curse on the people of God. But when Balaam opened his mouth to curse Israel, out came a blessing. Listen carefully to what Balaam said:

Numbers 23:

8 "How shall I curse, whom God hath not cursed? or how shall I defy, whom the Lord hath not defied?"

9 "For from the top of the rocks I see him, and from the hills I behold him: lo, the people shall dwell alone, and shall not be reckoned among the nations."

10 "Who can count the dust of Jacob, and the number of the fourth part of Israel? Let me die the death of the righteous, and let my last end be like his!"

Instead of being a curse, this is one of the most interesting prophetic utterances concerning Israel we have in all the Word of God. Balaam specifically states that he can't curse those God has blessed.

"From the top of the rocks I see him, and from the hills I behold him; lo, the people shall dwell alone and shall not be reckoned among the nations"; Numbers 23:9.

This means the Jews will retain their pure Jewish line and will, in the main, refrain from intermarrying with gentiles. They will continue as Jews through all future time. Has history proved his prophetic word to be true? Indeed, it has. There will always be Jews, and they will be here when Jesus returns to this earth.

Balaam even makes a prophetic statement that at the end the Jews will be righteous believers and he wishes to share in their final destiny. You can understand why King Balak was infuriated by words like these from Balaam. He had brought the world's greatest curser to curse the Jews and here he was uttering prophetic words about their preservation and their ultimate salvation.

A second attempt is made to get Balaam to curse Israel but we read in Numbers 23:20, "Behold, I have received commandment to bless: and he [God] hath blessed; and I cannot reverse it."

The beautiful prophecy about the preservation flows on and is climaxed with Verse 24. "Behold, the people shall rise up as a great lion, and lift up himself as a young lion: he shall not lie down until he eat of the prey, and drink the blood of the slain."

It was almost more than Balak could stand. One last attempt was made, from another mountain peak, to get Balaam to curse Israel. However, the third blessing surpassed anything Balaam had spoken before.

Numbers 24:

17 "I shall see him, but not now: I shall behold him, but not nigh: there shall come a Star out of Jacob, and a Sceptre shall rise out of Israel, and shall smite the corners of Moab, and destroy all the children of Sheth."

18 "And Edom shall be a possession, Seir also shall be a possession for his enemies; and Israel shall do valiantly."

19 "Out of Jacob shall come he that shall have dominion, and shall destroy him that remaineth of the city."

This is a prophecy of the coming of Jesus. From that mountaintop Balaam told Balak that eventually Christ would be born and the Jews would overrun Moab. The overruling will of God had prevailed. And as we look back on more than three thousand years of history, we see that the prophetic words of Balaam have been fulfilled and will one day be completely fulfilled. Look at Numbers 24:25. "And Balaam rose up, and went and returned to his place: and Balak also went his way." It appears that Balaam returned to his faraway northern home, but he didn't. He remained in Moab to see what would happen to the Jews.

A Disastrous Suggestion

Even though Balaam was not permitted to curse Israel, he did make a suggestion to Balak which almost destroyed Israel. He told Balak to pick out

34

the most beautiful girls and women of Moab and send them down into the camp of Israel. This Balak did, and the immorality that resulted got the minds of Israel off their main objective and had it not been for the grace of God Israel would have been annihilated there and never would have gotten into Canaan.

The End Of Balaam

Even though Balaam was a believer, as we have established above, he was a disobedient believer and he died the sin unto death. The sin unto death is a sin that only a believer can commit. It is a sin that comes to a man who refuses to do the will of God and continues in disobedience to the point of no return. God is left no alternative except to let the disobedient believer go so far that nothing but death can end his rebellion. You witnessed this in the death of King Saul as he repeatedly tried to kill David. The last phrase of Numbers 31:8 records the death of Balaam. "Balaam also the son of Beor they slew with the sword." He actually fought with the Army of Moab against Israel and God permitted him to die in that way.

The Geographical Will Of God

There is a fourth will of God that we see demonstrated in this great lesson. God did not want Balaam in Moab. He should have stayed as far away from Moab as possible, but the temptation of a big reward was too much for Balaam. The definite and clear will of God said, "Stay out of Moab," but Balaam wanted that reward and God permitted him to go.

The lesson we are to learn from this story is that God has a geographical will for every one of us. If God wants you in Jerusalem, then he doesn't want you in Rome. If God sends you to the west, then you can't expect to do God's will by going east. For example, in Genesis 12:1 God told Abraham, "Get thee out of thy country..." It is quite clear that the geographical will of God for Abraham was not Ur, in Southern Mesopotamia near the Persian Gulf, but was the land of Canaan — and God has a geographical will for every one of his own in every stage of his life. Jonah could not find the geographical will of God in Ninevah in the east as long as he persisted in going west on that ship. And Paul could not find the geographical will of God in Jerusalem since God wanted him to go on to the west into Spain from Rome.

The Four Wills Of God

Look at the four wills of God that stretch out before you.
1. The definite direct will of God.
2. The permissive will of God. (Quite clearly, this is not the best thing for you.)
3. The overruling will of God. (God always knows best and will not permit you to defeat his plan for the ages.)
4. The geographical will of God.

The Highest Will Of All

The definite and direct will of God is the best and safest place for any person to reside. When Christ was facing the cross, which was the crowning event of God's eternal plan, he faced it with the words we find in Mark 26:39: "And he went a little farther, and fell on his face, and prayed, saying, O my Father, if it be possible, let this cup pass from me: nevertheless not as I will, but as thou wilt."

That "nevertheless" was the greatest nevertheless of history. It changed the course of all history. Yes, it is true, "To find the will of God is the greatest discovery." Have you found that will for your life?

Personal Note

As I have just closed the last paragraph of this chapter I looked back over more than forty years of service as a B.S.U. secretary and a pastor of churches. I recall the dilemma I faced in the closing months of my Seminary training. I had prepared to become a preacher and a pastor, but no place of service had opened up to me. Then one day I received three letters in the same mail. One letter opened the door for me to consider a church in Mississippi. Another letter invited me to visit Washington, D.C. and consider the task of an associate pastor under a much older minister. The third letter came from Missouri inviting me to become the Baptist Student Secretary for that state. Here were three opportunities for service and I knew I could not accept them all. I was literally in a traffic jam of wills, and I did not know the way to go. I recall how I took those letters to my place of prayer for about a week and I openly placed them before the Lord. Which way should I go? By the end of the week my answer was clear. Almost as if God had spoken in an audible voice, and almost as if he had written in red ink across that letter from Missouri, he gave me the message, "This Is It!" Twice since then God has used those same three words to speak into the ears of my mind. The verse I had long before learned had become a reality, "This is the way, walk ye in it; when you turn to the right hand and when you turn to the left."

VI

UNDERSTANDING THE OLD SIN NATURE

Every member of the human race has an Old Sin Nature; however, Jesus Christ did not have an old sin nature because of his unique birth. As we develop this study we will return to this concept and show how Christ avoided having an old sin nature by being born of Mary without a human father.

The Makeup Of The Soul

Man's soul was created by God and placed inside man. Your soul is the real you. Soul and Spirit are different, as indicated by Hebrews 4:12: "For the Word of God is alive and powerful, sharper than any two-edged sword, piercing even to dividing asunder of the soul and the spirit, and the joints and the marrow, and is a discerner of the thoughts and intents of the heart."

The makeup of the soul is as follows:

Self-consciousness
Mentality
Volition
Conscience
Emotion
Old Sin Nature (the part man added)

The Old Sin Nature Is The Source Of Spiritual Death

Romans 5:12 says, "Wherefore, as by one man sin entered into the world, and death by sin; and so death passed upon all men, for that all have sinned [when Adam sinned]." Almost every time you see the word "sin" in the singular it refers to the old sin nature. When this verse says "sin entered into the world" it is referring to the old sin nature.

Adam And Eve Were Created Without An Old Sin Nature, But They Got One When They Ate Of The Forbidden Fruit

When the woman ate of the forbidden fruit in the Garden of Eden she immediately received an old sin nature. She gave the fruit to her husband, Adam, and he ate of the fruit and he, too, received an old sin nature. Though they both committed the same sin and they both became sinners in the same way, God held the man responsible. As a result of this, the old sin nature comes down through the seed of the man and not through the seed of the woman. The reason for this is that the woman was deceived when she ate of the fruit. She didn't have a clear idea of the meaning of her sinful act. But when Adam ate of the forbidden fruit the woman offered him, he did so deliberately. And he fully understood the implications of what he had done.

37

Paul explains this quite clearly in 1 Timothy 2:14: "And Adam was not deceived, but the woman being deceived, was in the transgression." This means the woman became a sinner just as Adam did, but God did not hold her responsible for her act. The responsibility for sin fell on Adam. That is why in 1 Corinthians 15:22 Paul wrote: "For as in Adam all die, even so in Christ shall all be made alive."

Christ's Birth Was Unique

When Christ was born his birth was unique. Every other person had been born from the seed of a man plus the seed of a woman. But when Christ was born, God the Holy Spirit planted a seed in Mary's body and the child was born from the seed of the woman without the seed of the man. Since you get your old sin nature from the male seed, Jesus was born without an old sin nature. During the more than thirty years he spent on the earth he never committed an act of sin. Therefore, by not having an old sin nature and by never committing an act of sin, Paul could write in 2 Corinthians 5:21: "For he hath made him to be sin for us, who knew no sin; that we might be made the righteousness of God in him."

This is why the first reference in the Bible to the person of Christ refers to him as "the seed of the woman." Genesis 3:15 says: "And I will put enmity between thee [Satan] and the woman, and between thy seed and her seed; it [Jesus] shall bruise thy head [Satan], and thou [Satan] shall bruise his [Jesus'] heel." In this passage Jesus is referred to as the seed of the woman. Therefore, Genesis 3:15 is a prophecy of his virgin birth as foretold in Isaiah 7:14 and quoted in Matthew 1:23. Jesus was born of a woman, without a father; therefore, he had no old sin nature. This was a unique birth. It happened once, and it will never happen again.

The Old Sin Nature Is Perpetuated In The Human Race
By Physical Birth

When Adam and Eve became sinners in the Garden of Eden, they set the stage for every member of the human race to be born with an old sin nature. The newborn baby does not have to commit an act of sin to become a sinner because that baby was born with an old sin nature. (The baby is protected by the grace of God until the age of responsibility is reached, then the child becomes responsible to God for his own acts. If a baby dies before that time, that baby will spend eternity with God because of the grace of God, as per II Samuel 12:22 and 23.) Adam and Eve were created innocent and they ate the forbidden fruit and acquired an old sin nature. But from that moment on every person born was born with an old sin nature. (This is known as the doctrine of total depravity.) David said in Psalm 51:5: "I was shapen in sin and in sin did my mother conceive me." David didn't mean that his mother committed a sin in the act of his conception, but rather that he was born with an old sin nature.

The lack of an old sin nature sets Christ apart from all other members of the human race. He is the only human being ever born without an old sin nature. This is why the virgin birth is so important, or perhaps we should call it the virgin conception. The seed was from God and not from a man, and when that baby was born of Mary in Bethlehem, he was born without an old sin nature. That is why the writer of Hebrews in Hebrews 2:14 wrote, "Forasmuch then as the children are partakers of flesh and blood, he also himself likewise took part of the same..." That "part of the same" refers to our humanity, minus the old sin nature.

The Believer Continues To Have An Old Sin Nature After Salvation

John says in 1 John 1:8 (and he was writing to believers): "If we [believers] say that we have no sin [old sin nature], we deceive ourselves, and the truth is not in us." Please notice that in this verse the word is in the singular and it means old sin nature. When Paul wrote to the young Christians in Corinth he said to them in 1 Corinthians 3:1: "And I, brethren [meaning believers] could not speak unto you as spiritual, but as unto carnal, even as unto babes in Christ." These were young converts, but they were allowing the old sin nature to dominate them and they were carnal. This is why the believer, under the control of the old sin nature, will commit the same kind of sins he would have committed had he never been saved at all. In fact, he might even sin with greater intensity because he now has more barriers to overcome and more impediments to step over. The old sin nature in a believer can only be held in check by the power of the Holy Spirit within the believer and by the intake of the Word of God.

The Old Sin Nature Frustrates Bona Fide Production
In The Christian Life

The Christian is equipped to produce divine good but the old sin nature frustrates this production and causes the believer to produce human good. This human good is the wood, hay and stubble Paul talks about in 1 Corinthians 3:12. The gold, silver and precious stone is divine good. Everything a believer does while he is controlled by the Holy Spirit is divine good. (This is when he is in the bottom circle of our diagram on Page 7.) Everything a person does when he is out of that bottom circle and is controlled by the old sin nature is human good. All the human good of believers will be burned at the judgment seat of Christ. A believer cannot pray while he is out of fellowship and while he is controlled by the old sin nature. The Psalmist says in Psalm 66:18: "If I regard iniquity in my heart, the Lord will not hear me."

The Old Sin Nature Is Called By Many Names In Scripture

a. **The Flesh.** Quite often the old sin nature is called "The flesh." In Galatians 5:16 Paul says: "This I say then, walk in the spirit, and ye shall not fulfill the lusts of the flesh."

b. **The Old Man.** In Ephesians 4:22 Paul calls the old sin nature "The old man." "That ye put off concerning the former conversation the old man, which is corrupt according to the deceitful lusts." In Colossians 3:9 he says: "Lie not one to another, seeing that ye have put off the old man with his deeds."

c. **Carnal.** We have mentioned this above, but this is one of the most familiar names given the old sin nature in scripture. In Romans 7:14 Paul says, "For we know that the law is spiritual: but I [old sin nature] am carnal, sold under sin."

d. **Sin in the Singular.** When you see the word "sin" in the singular, you can know that almost every time it is referring to the old sin nature and not to some act of sin. For example, Romans 5:12: "Wherefore, as by one man sin entered into the world, and death by sin; and so death passed upon all men, for that all have sinned." 1 John 1:8: "If we say that we have no sin, we deceive ourselves, and the truth is not in us." 1 Corinthians 15:56: "The sting of death is sin; and the strength of sin is the law."

The Solution To The Problem Of The Old Sin Nature

Christ went to the cross and the old sin nature of man was judged. Christ rejected human good and judged all our sins on the cross. After we become believers the acts of the old sin nature are judged by confession. 1 John 1:9 is vitally important here. We confess the acts of our old sin nature, God forgives us and restores us to fellowship. The unbeliever does not have access to 1 John 1:9 and he carries the guilt of his sin, which we call human good, and all human good of the unbeliever will be judged at the great white judgment throne according to Revelation 20:12 and 13.

There Will Be No Old Sin Nature In The Resurrection Body Of A Believer

Every believer will stand at the judgment seat of Christ in his resurrection body and the old sin nature will be stripped away and all his human good will be burned. 1 John 3:2: "Beloved, now are we the sons of God, and it doth not yet appear what we shall be: but we know that, when he shall appear, we shall be like him; for we shall see him as he is." This doesn't mean we will look like Christ. It means we will be like him in that we will not have our old sin nature.

The Old Sin Nature Defined

I cannot close this study on the old sin nature without looking at two scriptures. Romans 5:12: "Wherefore as by one man [Adam] sin [old sin nature] entered into the world, and death by sin [old sin nature]; and so death passed on all men, for that all have sinned [when Adam sinned]." The other scripture that is so vital in an understanding of the old sin nature is John 16:8 and 9. "And when he [the Holy Spirit] is come he will convict the

world of sin [notice it is in the singular] and of righteousness and of judgment: of sin [in the singular], because they believe not on me." The most
terrible sin the old sin nature inspires is failure to believe in Jesus Christ.
Satan uses the old sin nature to keep the unbeliever from accepting him.

VII

REPENTANCE AS TAUGHT BY JOHN THE BAPTIST

In the opening statement of Matthew 3 we find these words: "In those days came John the Baptist preaching in the wilderness of Judea, and saying, Repent ye: for the kingdom of heaven is at hand." It is very unfortunate that almost the entire Christian world has misunderstood the impact of these words of John. "Repent ye" to most all of the Christian World means to repent of your sins, turn from your sins, be sorry for your sins! Let me suggest, by contrast, that "repent" is a transitive verb and that it has a subject and an object. The subject is the one doing the repentance, and the object is not sin, but Jesus Christ. No unsaved man can repent of his sins. If an unsaved man could repent of his sins, there would be no reason for the salvation which Christ and only Christ can provide. For the unsaved man repentance is always beamed toward Christ, not toward sin. Repentance means a change of mental attitude and the mental attitude is directed toward Christ. This is precisely the theme of the preaching of John the Baptist as recorded in Matthew 3.

A Four-Fold Message

As we attempt to understand repentance as John preached it, let us first look at the four fundamental truths John preached. First, John 1:29, "The next day John seeth Jesus coming unto him, and saith, Behold the Lamb of God, which taketh away the sin of the world." For centuries, the Jews had been putting lambs on altars as a part of their worship, but the ritual had become commonplace to them and they had lost the reality of the sacrifice of a lamb on an altar. John appeared and pointed to Jesus and said, "Look, this is **The** Lamb of God, this one, Jesus Christ, is the true lamb and is the fulfillment of the whole Levitical sacrificial system. Christ is God's lamb that is to be sacrificed on a cross whereby atonement will be made for every sin of every man of the whole human race." Therefore, the preaching of John was the preaching of identification. He pointed to Jesus with an identifying finger and said, "This is the true Lamb of God, and he has come to die for our sins."

The second emphasis of John's preaching is found in John 3:30. "He must increase, but I must decrease." John's ministry was a short ministry and was a decreasing, declining ministry. But the ministry of the Son of God was an increasing, enlarging ministry which would grow into an everlasting kingdom which will abide forever and ever. This characteristic of John points the way for every believer to come to the place where he can say, "I am nothing, but Christ is everything."

43

The third emphasis of the preaching of John is found in the two words "Repent ye." Repent comes from the Greek verb **meta noeo** and means "change your mind, change your mental attitude." For the unsaved man it always means "change your mind about Christ." It is the negative side of "believe." Believe and repent mean exactly the same thing: One is positive and the other is negative. You can't believe without repenting, and you can't repent without believing; therefore, "Repent ye" clarifies the issue. The issue is not sin; the issue is Christ. Once this issue is settled, the new believer (with Christ and the Holy Spirit within him) goes out into the world and begins his life-long battle with sin. This he does by means of confession as outlined in 1 John 1:9.

Finally, the basic emphasis of John's preaching was contained in these words: "Believe on the Lord Jesus Christ and thou shalt be saved." Paul stated this in Acts 19:4 as he explained the essence of the preaching of John to the Corinthians.

Salvation And The Confession Of Sins (After Salvation)

Matthew 3:3: "For this is he that was spoken of by the prophet Esaias, saying, The voice of one crying in the wilderness, Prepare ye the way of the Lord, make his paths straight." This is one of the clearest explanations in the Word of God of salvation and the confession of sins after salvation.

Salvation — "Prepare ye the way of the Lord."

Confession — "Make his paths straight."

Now, how do we know that "prepare ye the way of the Lord" means salvation, and "make his paths straight" refers to confession of sins? The reason we know this comes from the **tense** of the Greek verbs used in these statements. "Prepare ye" is the aorist, active, imperative of the Greek verb **hetoimazo.** The aorist tense refers to a point of time when one believes in Christ. We have a song which says "The way of the cross leads home." This is correct theology and refers to a point of time when one believes in Christ and is saved. "The way of the cross" in the song is exactly the same as "The way of the Lord" in Matthew 3:3. The active voice of **hetoimazo** means that every person must believe for himself. No one can do this for him. He must do it for himself. The imperative mood means that this is a command from God. It is not optional. It is an absolute necessity if one is to be saved. Therefore, "Prepare ye the way of the Lord" is an idiomatic expression for the act of salvation. Every time a new convert believes in Christ he has "prepared the way of the Lord." It happens once, in a point of time, and it can never happen again.

The Koine Greek is the most exact language in the history of man, and this verse is a beautiful example of this fact. We have just seen the aorist tense of "prepare ye the way of the Lord" as a once and for all happening. Next we

44

come to the phrase, "Make his paths straight," and this is a present, active, imperative. The present tense refers to something you do over and over again. Every time you sin you confess your sins and get back in fellowship with God (get back in the bottom circle as in the diagram on Page 7). Therefore, "Make his paths straight" is a daily occurrence, or an occurrence just as often as sin touches your life. The active voice means you must confess your own sins. No one can do it for you. The imperative mood means this is a command from God and is not optional.

You handle your sins after salvation. Please note very carefully the sequence we have here. Belief in Christ always comes before the confession of sins. You cannot confess your sins and then believe; you believe and then confess. Confession of sins is for believers only! Confession of sins is a post-salvation experience. You prepare the way of the Lord (salvation); then you make his paths straight (confession of sins). One is a once-and-for-all experience (aorist tense), while the other is a daily occurrence (present tense).

Two Post-Salvation Experiences

Matthew 3:6: "And were baptized of him in Jordan, confessing their sins." Here in this verse, John the Baptist outlines two post-salvation experiences: one is Baptism and the other is the confession of sins. Baptism is a ritual through which the new believer goes to picture his identification with Jesus Christ. It is a double identification. As he is put under the water, he is identified with Christ in his death. The new believer is under the water, he can't breathe, and if he stayed there he would die. But it is also an identification with Christ on the cross, when he died for the sins of the world. Therefore, in baptism the believer travels all the way back to the cross and is identified with Christ in his death.

But the next moment, the new convert is brought out of the water and is identified with the air, and can breathe, and is identified with Christ in his ever-living resurrection life. Therefore, the baptism of the new believer is a double identification, an identification with death and an identification with life. Here in this verse, Matthew 3:6, "Baptized" is in the imperfect tense and this means they just kept coming to be baptized. Some believed today and were baptized and then some believed the next day and were baptized. As long as they kept coming, John kept on baptizing them. This is the meaning of the imperfect tense of this Greek verb **baptizo.**

The words "confessing their sins" are the present tense of the Greek verb **homo logeo** and mean that as often as they sinned they confessed. God looked at the cross and said, "Yes, my Son atoned for that sin on the cross, and you have been man enough to acknowledge it, to name it, to confess it, so all I can do is forgive it."

45

John Refused Baptism For Some

Matthew 3:7: "But when he saw many of the Pharisees and Sadducees come to his baptism, he said unto them, O generation of vipers, who hath warned you to flee from the wrath to come?" In this verse you notice that while John was baptizing his new converts in the Jordan, he looked up one day and there stood some of the Pharisees and Sadducees in line offering themselves as baptismal candidates. That is the meaning of the words, "come to his baptism." But John refused to baptize them. Why? They were religious. They were the Pharisees and the Sadducees. They were involved with all of the ritual of religion in the Temple of Jerusalem, but they had ritual without reality. They wanted the ritual of religion without the reality of salvation. They had ritual without regeneration. By refusing to baptize them, John was saying to them as loudly as he could, "You must be born again."

VIII

NOT BY BREAD ALONE

One day when John the Baptist was baptizing those who responded to his message by believing in Christ, he looked up and saw Christ standing in line waiting to be baptized. At first, John refused to baptize Christ, saying, "I have need to be baptized of thee." Jesus replied, "Suffer it to be so now: for thus it becometh us to fulfill all righteousness." The word, "suffer," is the aorist, active, imperative of the Greek verb **aphiemi,** and it actually means "I command you to baptize me." Therefore, when John realized Jesus had given him a direct command, he promptly obeyed.

This brings into focus the question, "Why was Jesus baptized, and what was the significance of this baptismal act for him?" The answer lies in the meaning of the Greek word **baptizo,** which has not been translated but simply transliterated and brought over into our language. The true meaning of **baptizo** is identification. In our immersion in water the water represents our sinful condition before salvation. Therefore, we immerse the new convert in the water as a picture of his identification with his dead condition in sin. The next moment we bring the new convert up out of the water and he is identified with the air, he can breathe again, he is identified with life — a picture of his new condition because he is identified with Christ. Therefore, baptism is a physical picture of conversion and shows how the new believer has gone from death to life, from unbelief to belief, from a sinful state to a new life in Christ.

However, baptism for Jesus was entirely different. He had no life of sin or unbelief from which to turn, and his identification was entirely different from ours. In being identified with the water, he was saying publicly, "I am identified with the plan of God for my life. I will carry out the mission for which I was born. I will go to the cross." Therefore, the baptism of Jesus was unique. No one was ever baptized as he was, for no one else was qualified to go to the cross. This is why we read in Matthew 3:17 these words: "And lo a voice from heaven saying, This is my beloved Son, in whom I am well pleased. God was pleased because Christ had publicly declared in his baptism this fact: "I am identified with the Father's plan for my life. I will go to the cross and die for the sins of the world." Therefore, no one should ever say, "I will follow Christ in baptism." This is impossible, and it shows how little one knows about the meaning of Christ's baptism. We are baptized to picture our death to the old life of sin and unbelief and our new identity with life by faith in Christ. But Christ's baptism was unique just as his birth was

47

unique. In his baptism he was saying, "I am identified with the Father's plan for my life."

Immediately the Devil met Christ to tempt him. This brings into focus a great principle. Once we have a spiritual experience, the Devil attacks us with temptations. The Devil saw Christ baptized in which he affirmed his decision to go to the cross. Immediately the Devil flung a temptation before him. Matthew 4:1 says, "Then was Jesus led up of the Spirit into the wilderness to be tempted of the Devil." This word "then" is an adverb of chronology from the Greek word **tote** and it means "Immediately." Therefore, we know Matthew 4 follows chronologically the events of Matthew 3, with nothing intervening.

To understand the temptations, there are certain doctrines we must understand concerning the person of Christ. One of those doctrines is what we call the doctrine of Christ's hypostatic union.

1. Jesus Christ has two natures. He is deity, and he is also humanity. He is undiminished deity and true humanity in one person forever. As deity, he is all that God is. He is sovereignty, righteousness, justice, eternal life, love, omniscience, omnipotence, omnipresence, immutability, and veracity. As a human, he is body, soul, and spirit, but he lacks an old sin nature. He was indwelt and sustained in his humanity by the Holy Spirit. As God, he is equal with God the Father, and God the Holy Spirit. As humanity, he is true humanity and superior to all other human beings in that he had no old sin nature and never committed an act of sin.

2. The Impeccability of Christ.
   In his deity, Christ could not be tempted, and he could not sin. God is perfect, and God cannot sin. From the standpoint of his humanity he could be tempted but he could not sin. Christ did not have an old sin nature, as has already been delineated in an earlier chapter. In this way he was like the first Adam. The first Adam was created innocent without an old sin nature. The second Adam, Jesus Christ, came into this world without an old sin nature through the virgin birth. It was the virgin birth that set Christ apart from the whole human race. Therefore, the first Adam and Jesus Christ started out in exactly the same way and were tempted under the same concept. Both were tempted by Satan to get them to use their own volition to act independently of God. With the first Adam, Satan was successful, but with the second Adam, totally unsuccessful. It was possible for Christ to be tempted in his humanity but at no point did he succumb to any temptation. We have a great verse of scripture that explains this. "Forasmuch then as the children are partakers of flesh and blood, he also himself likewise took part of the same..." Hebrews 2:14. "Part of the same" means he had a humanity like ours, yet

48

minus the old sin nature. Also, in Hebrews 4:15 we read, "For we have not a high priest which cannot be touched, with the feeling of our infirmities, but was in all points tempted like as we are, yet without sin."

And remember this: he was not only tempted as we are, but far beyond anything we will ever know in temptations. He faced temptations we will never face, yet without sin. No one else has ever been tempted to turn stone into bread, for no one else can do that. But he could do it and it was a real temptation to him.

There is another doctrine we must understand in order to comprehend the significance of his temptation. We call it the doctrine of **kenosis.** Kenosis is a Greek word. This doctrine says that the Holy Spirit sustained Christ all through his earthly ministry. This means that when Christ walked on the earth in his humanity he voluntarily restricted his deity. He voluntarily restricted the independent use of certain of his divine attributes. He did not use his own divine attributes to act independently of God. In his humanity he relied on the power of the Holy Spirit rather than on the omnipotence of his deity. He had omnipotence but he would not use it independently of the Father's plan. Look at seven ways in which the Holy Spirit sustained the humanity of Christ.

1. The fact that the Holy Spirit would sustain his humanity was prophesied. (Isaiah 11:2 and 3, Isaiah 42:1, Isaiah 61:1 and 2.)
2. The Holy Spirit was given to Christ without measure. (John 3:34.)
3. The Holy Spirit guaranteed He would sustain Christ during his earthly ministry, beginning at his baptism. (Matthew 3:16.)
4. The Holy Spirit provided power for the humanity of Christ during his earthly ministry, including his miracles. (Matthew 12:18 compared with Matthew 12:28, Luke 4:14, 15 and 18.)
5. Jesus was guided by the Holy Spirit. (Matthew 4:1.)
6. The ministry of the Holy Spirit was discontinued during those last three hours on the cross when all alone he bore our sins. (Psalm 22:1, Matthew 27:46.) On the cross he screamed over and over again, "My God (addressed to God the Father), My God (addressed to God the Holy Spirit), Why hast thou forsaken me?"
7. The Holy Spirit along with God the Father participated in his resurrection. (Romans 8:11, 1 Peter 3:18.)

The First Temptation. Matthew 4:1, "Then was Jesus led up of the spirit into the wilderness to be tempted of the devil." The word "then" from **tote** is a particle of chronology. In other words, these temptations are in chronological order and come immediately after his baptism. Christ's decision that he would go to the cross and die for the sins of the world would immediately be tested. "To be tempted" is the aorist, passive, infinitive of the word **peirazo.**

49

This testing will last for a period of forty days. Only three of the temptations are recorded here, and they are unique. Hebrews 4:15 tells us that he was tempted in many ways and yet without sin. Also, Mark 1:13 and Luke 4:2 mention the fact that he was tempted many times. The passive voice of **peirazo** lets us know he received this temptation from Satan and the infinitive lets us know it was Satan's purpose to keep Christ from going to the cross if he could.

After fasting for forty days, Christ was exceedingly hungry. I think we should make a distinction here between fasting and dieting. People diet to lose weight, but fasting is different. Fasting means that the usual time used for eating is going to be taken for meditation and prayer. True fasting includes study and prayer and meditation. Matthew 4:2 says that after 40 days of fasting "he was afterwards an hungered." This does not refer to his deity. Deity is never hungry, for deity owns all the food in the universe. This is a reference to his humanity.

Matthew 4:3, "And when the tempter came to him he said, If Thou be the Son of God, command that these stones be made bread." At this point I would like to give five principles with respect to this first temptation.

1. This first temptation dealt with the relationship with the Holy Spirit which indwelt Christ.
2. Here in this temptation Christ was being asked to act independently of the Holy Spirit within.
3. The temptation was designed to get Christ to violate the kenosis principle. He was tempted to reach over into his omnipotence and use his divine power to feed himself and not rely on the Holy Spirit to sustain him.
4. This is a temptation that could only apply to Christ. It would not apply to us because we cannot turn stone into bread, but Christ could do this; therefore, this was a very real temptation to Christ. We could anoint a stone with oil, pray over it or even speak in tongues over it and it would not turn into bread. But to Christ, this was no problem at all. He could wave his hand over a stone or even a whole mountain and both the stone and the mountain would be turned into bread.
5. In principle, we face the same temptation. We are constantly tempted to rely on our old sin nature rather than to rely on the power of the Holy Spirit. Christ could reach back and use the power of his omnipotence, or he could rely on the power of the Holy Spirit to sustain him.

The words, "When the tempter came" is a present, active, participle and should read "When the one who constantly tempts came to him." "If Thou be the Son of God" is a first class condition and it means "If Thou be the Son of God, and you are." We could read this "Since you are the Son of God." Satan and all angelic beings, including all demons, recognize the fact that

Jesus is the Son of God. "Command that these stones be made bread" is the aorist, active, imperative of the Greek word **epo,** and it means "Tell these stones to turn into bread."

1. Jesus was hungry in his humanity. It would have been very simple for the Son of God to do this. However, it was not a part of the Father's plan for Jesus to use his omnipotence to interfere with his humanity.
2. To turn stones into bread would be depending on his own volition rather than doing the will of the Father. Behind this refusal was this fact: Christ had not come to the earth to turn stone into bread but to turn sinful men into Sons of God.
3. Hence, in this first temptation the relationship of the humanity of Jesus to the indwelling Holy Spirit is here under test.
4. Furthermore, Jesus was being tempted to obtain a lawful thing (food) in an unlawful way, apart from the power of the Holy Spirit within him.
5. Also, Jesus was in this first temptation being tempted as to the sufficiency of the Grace provision of his Father to care for his daily needs. The question is this: "Can the Father provide the daily needs of Jesus Christ, or must Christ operate on his own?" In a similar way, we face this same test every day. Are we going to depend on the grace provision from God, or are we going to take things out of his hands and do it ourselves?
6. Must Jesus depend upon himself by turning stones into bread, or can he wait for the Father to provide for him? Christ knew he would not die until he got to the cross. Does he have patience to wait for the Father's plan to develop, or will he move ahead, taking things into his own hands?
7. This introduces the faith-rest issue. Are we willing to trust the Father, or are we going to take things into our hands and try to do it on our own?
8. God the Father will not allow Christ to starve to death. The Scriptures of the Old Testament are filled with passages that refer to the cross and how Christ will die on the cross. This first promise of his victory on the cross is stated in Genesis 3:15. Every Levitical altar that pictures an animal on the altar is a picture pointing to the Lamb of God who would one day die on the cross.

Isaiah 53 is a beautiful picture of Christ's atoning death. Jesus knew the Old Testament and he knew all of these passages that pointed to his death on the cross. Therefore, he knew that he would not starve to death, but would live to reach the cross.

Matthew 4:4: "But he answered and said, it is written, Man shall not live by bread alone, but by every word that proceedeth out of the mouth of God." Here Jesus is giving Satan a resounding "No" to his temptation, and Jesus used the Word of God whereby he would answer Satan. "He answered and said" is an expression that appears dozens of times in the gospels. "He answered" is an aorist, passive, participle and it means Christ received the answer to all these things in eternity past. "And said" is an aorist, active, indicative and means that now in time he will speak the correct answer. Christ not only gave him an answer, he gave him a dogmatic answer. The answer is a quotation of Deuteronomy 8:3. "It is written" is a perfect tense in the Greek, and it means it was true when it was written and it will remain true forever. Victory comes through the word of God. "Man shall not live by bread alone." The word "alone" means that life is so constituted that food is a necessity.

1. Bread or physical food is necessary for physical life, but it is a mere detail in man's dependence upon God.
2. It isn't the food but the promise from God that guarantees the food that really counts. The promises of God abide. The promises of God sort out what is important from the mere details of life.
3. While bread is necessary to sustain life, it is a mere detail for survival.
4. The force that really sustains man is the promises of God. Remember, as long as you live you will have the promises of God.

Jesus then quoted the words, "But by every word that proceedeth out of the mouth of God." "Proceedeth out" is the present, active, participle of the Greek verb **ekporeuomai,** and it should be translated "that keeps on coming out of the mouth of God." In other words, the Word of God is eternal and will abide forever. Therefore, the pattern for resisting temptation is as follows:

1. Reliance on the Word of God is the basis for spiritual victory.
2. All spiritual victory in the life of a Christian is related to the Word of God and the doctrine contained therein.
3. Jesus never put his own power or his own works on the same level with obedience to the Father's plan. Therefore, he obeyed the Father's plan by using the Word of God and by depending on the power of the Holy Spirit.
4. Jesus found his greatest strength, therefore, not in performing a miracle, but in obeying the Word of God.
5. Dependence on God and fulfilling the plan of God depends on knowing the Word of God.

Christ, having defeated the Devil in the first temptation, was immediately tested in another realm. The key to the first temptation is the Holy Spirit. The Key to the second temptation is the Word of God. The key to the third temptation is the plan of God the Father for Christ's life.

The Second Temptation. Matthew 4:6: "And saith unto him, If thou be the Son of God, cast thyself down: for it is written, He shall give his angels charge concerning thee: and in their hands they shall bear thee up, lest at any time thou dash thy foot against a stone." The second temptation occurred from the pinnacle of the Temple in Jerusalem. This second temptation deals with our relationship to the Word of God. Since Jesus resisted the first temptation by quoting the Word of God, Satan now attacks the source, which is the Word itself. Satan will attack the Word by quoting it, distorting it, and by using a passage which was not pertinent to the situation. The Devil will distort the Scripture by using it out of context.

The location for this second temptation was from a porch which had been built by Herod the Great as an addition to Solomon's temple. From that vantage point it was over 400 feet down to the Kidron Valley below. The Devil began the second temptation just as he had begun the first: "Since you are the Son of God cast thyself down." In other words, he said to Jesus, "Jump!" But deity can't jump, because in his deity he was already down there and everywhere else. In his deity he already was everywhere; therefore, this command to jump applied only to his humanity.

1. To jump into the valley without injury would violate the law of gravity. The law of gravity is a divine law, and in his humanity Christ was living under that law.
2. God does not protect the operation of negative volition in defiance of divine law. Christ had free will, and if he acted negatively violating a divine law, he would remove himself from divine protection.
3. If someone had pushed Christ over the cliff, then God would have protected him. But if he jumped of his own volition, he would have been killed.

Dashing thy foot against a stone is an idiom used here for falling. But the Devil added the words, "Lest at any time." This is a quotation of Psalm 91:11-12 and "Lest at any time" is not a part of that passage.

1. These words were added by Satan.
2. Satan added these words so he could distort the whole passage.
3. There are times when God's protection is provided.
4. However, when a believer uses his volition to violate God's law and acts independently of God's will, then he places himself outside the protection of God.
5. For Jesus to have jumped would have been certain death for his humanity. Naturally his deity would not have died because deity cannot die. Even on the cross his deity didn't die; only his humanity.
6. It was not the will of God for Jesus to jump. It was the Father's will for him to die on the cross some three years later. Jesus refused to use his volition independently of the Father's will. This is what the first man and woman did in the Garden of Eden and, this is where the problem of sin began.

The answer of Jesus was quick and pointed. He quoted Deuteronomy 6:16, reminding Satan that he should never tempt the Lord God.

1. The issue was not to jump at Satan's command, but was instead never to tempt the Lord God.
2. Satan quoted scripture which did not apply. He quoted scripture out of context and also added to scripture. Jesus quoted scripture that did apply.
3. If Jesus had jumped, he would have committed suicide in his humanity. This reminds us that the date of our departure from this earth is in the hands of God and we are never to end our lives sooner than the Father's plan dictates. Job 5:26 is a great scripture that pertains to this truth.

The Third Temptation. Matthew 4:8-9: "Again, the devil taketh him up into an exceeding high mountain, and sheweth him all the kingdoms of the world, and the glory of them; And saith unto him, All these things will I give thee, if thou wilt fall down and worship me." For this temptation Satan took Christ into a high mountain and showed him all the kingdoms of the world. This third temptation deals with the believer's relationship to the Father's plan. It was the plan of the Father that Jesus would one day rule the world, but the Father's plan called for the cross to come before the crown. In establishing God's permanent kingdom of regenerated believers, Christ will not accept the rulership of the world on the Devil's schedule or the Devil's plan. If Jesus had accepted the Devil's offer, which was a bona fide offer, he would have bypassed the cross. The Devil hated the cross and did everything in his power to keep Christ from going there. The Devil knew that once Christ died on the cross, salvation would be completed. Christ gave a resounding "No" to the Devil's offer. It is rather interesting that the Beast of Revelation 13:1-10 will accept the Devil's offer, but Christ will return just in time to see that such a plan is never carried out.

The Reply of Christ. Matthew 4:10: "Then saith Jesus unto him, Get thee hence, Satan: for it is written, Thou shalt worship the Lord thy God, and him only shalt thou serve." These words, "Get thee hence" are far too mild to give us the actual meaning of Christ's reply to Satan's offer. Jesus actually said, "Get out of here." And the glorious thing is that the Devil obeyed. Jesus rebuffed Satan by quoting Deuteronomy 6:13. The only one to whom we bow or worship is Jesus Christ.

Matthew 4:11: "Then the devil leaveth him, and, behold, angels came and ministered unto him." This is always the result when we meet Satan with a firm reply and refuse to conform to his illegitimate demands.

THE GREATEST LOVE IN THE WORLD

John completed the writing of his Gospel in chapter twenty, and at the end of that chapter he recorded his reason for writing in the following words: "But these are written, that ye might believe that Jesus is the Christ, the Son of God; and that believing ye might have life through his name." John picked out certain signs and miracles to give emphasis to the fact that Jesus was the Messiah, the Son of God. It is quite clear that John had finished the message he intended to write. But very much as we sometimes write a letter and after finishing have something else important we want to say, we add what we call a P.S. I call John 21 the P.S. of John's gospel, and it is in this chapter where we have a beautiful description of the greatest love in the world.

Jesus made seventeen resurrection appearances prior to his ascension, and the appearance recorded here in John 21 is his third appearance to his disciples. The chapter begins with the words, "After these things," and they refer to the events of the previous chapter. The first two appearances were on Sunday, one week apart. At the first appearance Thomas was missing, but a week later Thomas was present and experienced the reality of the resurrected Christ. Now this third appearance is different from the other two in that it occurred on the Sea of Galilee. The language in John 21:1, "Jesus showed himself," is an aorist, active, indicative of **phaneroo** and it means he showed himself in his resurrection body. John wrote this gospel later than the other gospel writers and by the time John wrote, the Sea of Galilee had come to be known as the Sea of Tiberias, named for Tiberias Caesar.

I think it is quite significant that the seven disciples who made this fishing trip to Galilee are all mentioned by name except two. I feel quite certain that the two not named were Philip and Andrew, for they also loved to fish. As I am writing these lines I have just returned from another trip to Israel and possibly the most exciting day of our stay in Israel was the day we spent on and around the beautiful Sea of Galilee. Every time we go there we eat the noon meal at Tiberias, and they always serve "Saint Peter's fish." In this way we are reminded of the big fisherman and of his love for this beautiful sea. Peter said to the other disciples, "I go a-fishing." The suggestion was so forceful, the confused and frustrated disciples agreed to go along. I think it is significant that their fishing trip was an effort in frustration because Jesus had made an appointment with them on a mountain and not at the sea. The Lord had also told them to go out and fish for men, but here they are, back at the old trade, fishing for fish. Their all-night fishing expedition produced no fish even though they were all masters in the fishing business. It seems to me this clearly illustrates the fallacy of Christian service which is done in the energy of the flesh. A whole night of serious fishing on Galilee which produced no fish would certainly seem to indicate that something had gone wrong.

John 21:4: "But when the morning was now come, Jesus stood on the shore: but the disciples knew not that it was Jesus." I love this verse very much for it teaches us so clearly that Jesus always appears when we need him most. The word translated "the morning was now come" is the Greek word **ginomai** and it really means the dawn, "to be coming on — the dawn sneaking upon them." The discouraged, defeated fishermen were making their way to the shore, knowing they had lived through a night of useless activity. In my student days I heard the late S. D. Gordon give a devotional talk to about two thousand students in one of our southwide conferences, and as he described these defeated fishermen he pictured them with this language: "Here they come, just at dawn, empty-boated, heavy-hearted, fishless-netted." But when the morning comes, Jesus always stands on the shore. Morning never comes to any man's life without Jesus there to meet his needs. In a very friendly but firm voice Jesus said to them, "Boys, have you any meat?" The word is **prosphagion** and it literally means "Are you face to face with eating."

John 21:6: "And he said unto them, Cast the net on the right side of the ship, and ye shall find. They cast therefore, and now they were not able to draw it for the multitude of fishes." This was a command from Christ. The word **ballo** is in the imperative mood and it was a command for them to throw out the nets again. "Ye shall find" is the future, active, indicative of **eurisko** and it meant they were certain to find fish. At the first throw of the net, the net was swarming with fish. It was such a remarkable catch, after a whole night of frustration, that they actually counted them, and John records that they caught a hundred and fifty-three (153).

Peter couldn't wait to get to the shore. He left the boat and the fish to the others, but he swam quickly to the shore and Jesus said to him, "Bring of the fish which ye have now caught." It was then that Peter turned back to the boat, pulled in the net and counted the fish. The verse ends with an amazing assertion — "And for all there were so many, yet was not the net broken." Quite often before their nets had broken, but now Christ was risen from the dead and this meant new power in fishing. They would go out into the world and cast their nets for men and their nets would not break. Before we get past it, I think we should pause a moment with Verse 9, "As soon then as they were come to land, they saw a fire of coals there, and fish laid thereon, and bread." Jesus knew they were heavy-hearted and discouraged and quite hungry after the whole night of frustration. With those hands fresh from the cross and the nail prints, he had prepared breakfast for them. Fish and bread prepared by Christ for his hungry men. Who could ever imagine that Christ was not interested in little things?

There in the dawn they stood, dripping wet from the sea, and Jesus wanted them to dine. Verse 12: "Jesus saith unto them, Come and dine. And none of the disciples durst ask him, Who art thou? knowing that it was the Lord." This word, "dine," is the aorist, active, imperative from which we get the English word "aristocrat." An aristocrat is one who can sit down at the table and have someone serve him. That's exactly what Christ was going to do for these hungry men. Verse 13: "Jesus then cometh, and taketh bread, and giveth them, and fish likewise." Notice the verbs here — cometh, taketh, and giveth. These are all present tense verbs and it means Jesus did the serving all by himself and of his own volition.

1. Every verb here is a verb of action — cometh, taketh, giveth. Jesus did all the work here, just as he did on the cross, and this is a picture of grace.
2. This is the basic meaning of grace. He does it all and we can do nothing.
3. Please notice Jesus provided everything for the breakfast — the fire, the bread, and the fish. Christ picked up the check for this meal in eternity past. The only thing the disciples provided was their presence and their appetite.
4. The disciples had to eat for themselves. Christ provides everything for us, but he can't eat for us. Every person must eat for himself, believe for himself, be stabilized for himself.

We now come to that paragraph in scripture which gives us the Bible's most beautiful picture of the meaning of love. Now I am quite aware of the fact that practically all the commentaries tell us that **agape** is the Greek word for Godly love, for the highest type of love in all the world. I will admit that **agape** is Godly love when God is the subject, as it is in John 3:16. Indeed, this verse says "For God so loved the world," and here **agapao** is Godly love. But what about John 3:19? "And this is the condemnation, that light is come into the world, and men loved darkness rather than light, because their deeds were evil." Here **agapao** is used with the unbeliever in the phrase "men loved darkness." Here **agapao** is used with the unbeliever and therefore it cannot mean Godly love. I believe rather that **agape** love is better described as mental attitude love. God has a mental attitude love for the entire world. There has never been a man in the world who was not the recipient of the love of God. God loved Moses, but he loved Pharaoh no less. God loved John and Peter and Andrew but he loved Judas no less. God's great mental attitude love reaches out to every man and this I believe is the meaning of **agapao.**

In John 21:15-17 we have a beautiful description of the highest type of love in the world and I wish to suggest that this highest type of love is **phileo** love rather than **agape** love. Look with me at this amazing truth. Verse 15, "So when they had dined, Jesus saith to Simon Peter, Simon, son of Jonas, lovest thou me more than these? He saith unto him, Yea, Lord; thou knowest that I love thee. He saith unto him, Feed my lambs." In this verse Jesus said to Peter, "Lovest thou me?" and Jesus used the word **agapao.** It refers to mental attitude love. But Peter replied, "Yea, Lord, thou knowest that I love thee," and he used the word, **phileo.** I believe Peter was saying, "Lord, I more than **agapao** thee, I **phileo** thee. I love thee with that warm, personal love that can only come from knowing you and believing in you." Notice how Jesus responded to Peter's reply. He said, "Feed my lambs." The word for feed here is **bosko** and it is a present, active, imperative. The word for lambs is **arnion** and it means my baby lambs, my new converts. So the words together mean "keep on feeding my baby sheep, my new converts."

Verse 16, "He saith to him again the second time, Simon, son of Jonas, lovest thou me? He saith unto him, Yea, Lord, thou knowest that I love thee. He saith unto him, Feed my sheep." Jesus repeated his question and he stuck with his use of **agapao** for the word love. But notice Peter held his ground. Peter said in substance this, "Lord, I more than **agapao** thee. I **phileo** thee." He held to the word that means warm, personal, devoted love. Jesus replied by saying, "Feed my sheep," and this time the words are entirely different. The word for feed here is **poimaino** and it means, "Shepherd, discipline my sheep." The word for sheep here is **probaton** and it means "Shepherd my hard-headed sheep. Discipline my hard to control mature sheep."

Verse 17: "He saith unto him the third time, Simon, son of Jonas, lovest thou me? Peter was grieved because he said unto him the third time, Lovest thou me? And he said unto him, Lord, thou knowest all things; thou knowest that I love thee. Jesus saith unto him, Feed my sheep." The third time Jesus asked Peter, "Do you really **phileo** me? Have you come up to this high level of love? Peter do you really love me this much?" I believe this is why Peter was grieved when Jesus questioned his love. Three times Peter said, phileo, phileo, phileo. I think the history that follows proved Peter was right when he said he loved Jesus with the highest love possible. His preaching of the sermon on the day of Pentecost and his writing of 1st and 2nd Peter would be enough evidence to let us know this **phileo** love was the highest love known to man. This third time Jesus said to Peter, "Feed my sheep." The word for sheep is **probaton** and when we place these words together they mean "Feed my mature sheep, my growing sheep." There are three great commands here. "Feed my new converts, shepherd my hard-to-control sheep, feed my mature sheep." And to all three commands Peter responded by saying to his Lord, "I love thee as much as one man can love his Saviour and Lord." I believe Peter meant it. That's why I believe **phileo** love is the greatest love in the world. It includes **agape** love, mental attitude love, and adds a dimension of warm, personal contact love that comes from walking with the Lord and coming to know his word.

The Epilogue

There is a very beautiful ending to this visit by the blue waters of Galilee. Verse 18: "Verily, verily, I say unto thee, When thou wast young, thou girdedst thyself, and walkedst whither thou wouldest: but when thou shalt be old, thou shalt stretch forth thy hands, and another shall gird thee, and carry thee whither thou wouldest not." This verse actually predicts how Peter would die and how he would glorify the Lord in his death. And to bring it all to a climax, Jesus said to Simon, "Follow me." And the word is the present, active, imperative of **akoloutheo.** It means to walk along with someone who knows how to teach you and be a faithful student and learner. Peter will obey this command and his great doctrine in 1st and 2nd Peter shows just how faithful he was in diligent study of doctrinal truth.

Verse 20: "Then Peter, turning about, seeth the disciple whom Jesus loved following; which also leaned on his breast at supper, and said, Lord, which is he that betrayeth thee?" Verse 21: "Peter seeing him saith to Jesus, Lord, and what shall this man do?" Peter couldn't resist it. John was following along, listening to this interesting conversation between Jesus and Simon Peter. It was more than Peter could stand and he blurted out, "Jesus, what about John? What is he to do?" In substance, Jesus said, "Peter, that is none of your business. You follow me!" It is a lesson for all of us to learn. We are naturally interested in others, but our concern should never violate the volition of another. Each must answer for himself.

This golden chapter closes with another definite assertion that this is the perfect word of God. Verse 24, "This is the disciple which testifieth of these things, and wrote these things: and we know that his testimony is true." Let me add my personal word to John's dogmatic statement. I, too, can say, "We know this testimony is perfect truth."

THE ABSOLUTE CERTAINTY OF THE RESURRECTION

Corinth was one of the key centers of the world in the time of Christ and the early days of Christianity. Through the influence of Socrates and Plato in the Fifth Century B.C. the Greeks had come to believe that the ideal condition for the soul was to come to a time when their souls would be free, and by this they meant a soul liberated from the body. The Greeks regarded the body as a prison. The soul had all the responsibility and the body had none. They looked forward to death for at that time the soul would be liberated from the body. At death the Greeks believed they would cross the river Styx. Charon would ferry dead souls over the river encircling the lower world and they would be in a perfect place forever.

When Christ was preached to the Greeks some of them believed and Christian churches were started in various cities, including Corinth. But when Paul began to preach to them about the resurrection of the body, this idea cut across all they had been taught for centuries. They even began to regret that they had ever become Christians because for centuries the Greeks had been taught to look forward to the time when the soul would be free from the body. But once they had been saved they realized that they would live forever, and in addition to that, Paul came to them and preached to them the resurrection. They had come to understand the main points about living the Christian life on earth, but then Paul added the idea of the resurrection of the body. They learned that at death the soul and spirit would leave the body, and that suited their philosophy perfectly. They knew that there would be no more death, no more sorrow, and no more pain after the soul left the body. But when they heard, for the first time, that they were going to have a new body, they were thrown into great mental confusion. This is why it was necessary for Paul to write to them and attempt to straighten out their confused thinking about this subject. The Greeks were in danger of having a faith that was vain. They would need to be taught that a resurrection body was not something to be feared, but was something to which they should aspire. In order for Christians to grow they must know true doctrine, and the capstone of all Paul's preaching was the doctrine of the resurrection. Death apart from the resurrection is a disaster. So Paul set himself the task of writing information that would give the Greeks an accurate knowledge of life after death, including the resurrection body.

1 Corinthians 15:1: "Moreover, brethren, I declare unto you the gospel which I preached unto you, which also ye have received, and wherein ye

stand." This is addressed to born-again people — "Moreover, brethren." Paul would remind them at the outset that this doctrine of the resurrection was based on the new birth. Every member of the human race, except Christ, came into the world with a sinful nature. Adam and Eve were innocent at first, but once they sinned, they acquired an old sin nature, and since that moment every other person has been born with a sinful nature except Christ. Christ avoided this by being born of a virgin without having a human father. The old sin nature produces an area of weakness which produces sins. It also produces an area of strength which produces human good. But all our righteousnesses are as filthy rags in his sight, says Isaiah 64:6. When Christ went to the cross, he provided salvation for every man on the earth. Now if the plan of salvation is no stronger than man and what man can do, then that plan is weak and temporary and will not survive. But God designed a plan where God did all the work for salvation and we call this plan "GRACE." In 1 Corinthians 15:10 we find the words, "By the grace of God I am what I am." Grace is the principle by which we are born, by which we are converted, by which we live and by which we die, and by which one day we will receive a resurrection body. Christ provided the way of salvation on the cross and in that act all human good was rejected. There is no place in the plan of God for human good. This means that no one can be saved by going to church or by being baptized or by feeling sorry for his sins or by changing his behaviour pattern. The word **pisteuo,** which means faith, is a non-meritorious act. Scripture says, "Believe on the Lord Jesus Christ and thou shalt be saved" and this is why Paul starts here and says "Brethren." He is referring to people who are born again. Now, to be sure, all unsaved people are to experience the resurrection also; but Paul will explain that later on. He is here talking to born-again people and he calls them "Brethren."

Keep in mind the fact that men are not born equal and they don't become equal in achievement. There is no way for man by man's efforts to bring equality, brotherhood, world prosperity or world peace. Man can do certain things, but one thing he can't do is to make men equal. The only way for men to become equal is through regeneration and this solves the inequalities of the members of the human race. To be born into the family of God makes men equal, makes men brothers. By union with the Lord Jesus Christ we become the sons of God. That is why the scripture refers to neither bond nor free, neither male nor female. So this scripture is addressed to believers.

Once people become believers some distinctions begin to emerge in life's experiences. All of us start out in the Christian life equal, brothers. All begin as spiritual babies, and spiritual growth depends upon knowing and living by the Word of God. In Verse 2 Paul will speak of the faith of some believers as being "in vain." This doesn't mean that they were not saved, but that they haven't grown and appropriated doctrine to experience. These Corinthians were refusing to accept the doctrine of the resurrection and at that point their faith was in vain. Therefore, Paul had to begin with that part of the gospel they had already accepted and believed. They had received Christ as Saviour. But now Paul proceeded to preach a part of the gospel the Greek mind had difficulty accepting because of their training in centuries past. To the Greeks, getting out of the prison of the physical body was a great achievement and to put their saved souls back into another body was a terrible thing to the Greek mind.

Acts 17:31-32: "Because he hath appointed a day, in which he will judge the world in righteousness by that man whom he hath ordained; whereof he hath given assurance unto all man, in that he hath raised him from the dead. And when they heard of the resurrection of the dead some mocked: and others said, We will hear thee again of this matter." When Paul preached to the people of Athens on Mars Hill about the resurrection, it literally blew their minds apart, for they just couldn't imagine such a thing.

The words "I declare unto you" really mean "I make known unto you." "Unto you" is a dative of advantage, for it will be to their great advantage to hear this amazing truth. The word, "Gospel," means good news. It is good news that Christ paid the price for our salvation and that we can do nothing to merit it. "Which I preached" literally means "Which I have announced to you." The word "received" is from **paralambano. Para** is the preposition of immediate source, to receive from the immediate source of self. They heard the gospel and became positive toward the message, and on that positive volition they expressed their faith in Christ. The gospel is presented to unbelievers so they will be saved. The gospel is presented to believers so they will grow and orient themselves to the grace of God. The believer is saved and can't be saved again, but he can become oriented more completely to the grace of God.

Romans 8:32: "He that spared not his own Son, but delivered him up for us all, how shall he not with him also freely give us all things?" This verse shows us how we relate to the grace of God. If Christ did the most he could do for us while we were his enemies, what will he do for us now that we are his friends? In that case, he will do more than the most for us. So these Corinthians were under the "much more" grace of God. There are no problems too great for the plan of God. The words "wherein ye stand" should read "in the which ye stand." This is a perfect tense of the word stand and it means at the moment of salvation ye stand, and you will stand forever. Christianity is a relationship; it is not a religion.

Christ has eternal life and once we believe in him we share his eternal life. We share his heirship and his priesthood and his destiny. He is elected and we share his election. This is the basis for being in the top circle, for once you are saved you can't get out, no matter what you do. You can't lose your eternal life. The active voice of this verb means this is your very own possession. The indicative mood means the reality of your standing forever. There is no possible way to fall, no possible way to lose your salvation. There is no sin too great for the plan of God. The greatest pride one can have is to assume that one can commit a sin so great that by that act one can undo what Christ did for him in salvation. There is no disaster too great for eternal security. You will always be God's child once you are saved, no matter how you behave; and remember, God has had a great deal of experience in disciplining bad children. God knows how to deal with every disobedient child. So "wherein ye stand" means eternal security.

1 Corinthians 15:2: "By which also ye are saved, if ye keep in memory what I preached unto you, unless ye have believed in vain." At first glance this verse presents quite a problem, but it isn't if you know what the language means in the original text. It means "Through which Gospel you received salvation." This "if" is a first class condition and it means, "If you keep in memory what I preached unto you, and you do." He is reminding them that they carried over into their salvation the idea from Greek philosophy that the body was an evil thing and once the soul left the body, then the soul could be perfected. (To the Greeks the soul moved across the river Styx and into the peaceful and glorious Elysian fields. This appealed to the Greek mind but it was contrary to the teaching of scripture.) The words, "ye are saved," is a present, passive, indicative. The present tense refers to the dramatic moment of your salvation. The passive voice means that you received this salvation as a grace gift from God. The indicative mood means the reality of your salvation. This "if" is a first class condition and it means the statement is true. "If ye hold fast," and you do. Hold fast, or as translated here, "keep in memory," is from **katecho** and it means to hold something according to a norm or standard. So Paul will now add some additional doctrine for them to hold to. The world "unless" is used here as a first class condition of a debater's technique. He is using this phrase just so he can discuss the issue of the resurrection with them. They had crossed out the resurrection from their thinking, and thereby, were missing many blessings. The words, "in vain," mean "to no purpose." The real purpose was that so they could receive a blessing. This doesn't mean they were unsaved. One can be saved without believing in the resurrection, but if one properly understands the scripture, he will believe in the resurrection. But they had been so deeply steeped in their Greek teaching they had completely missed the blessing that can come from believing in the resurrection.

1 Corinthians 15:3: "For I delivered unto you first of all that which I also received, how that Christ dies for our sins according to the scriptures." "I

delivered unto you" means to give something from the immediate source of your self and is from **paradidomi.** "To you" is the dative of advantage. "That which I also received" means that on the Damascus Road and in his quiet "seminary days" in Arabia he met the resurrected Lord and knew he was alive. Paul received his message directly from Jesus Christ. "How that Christ died" is from **apothenesko. Apo** means from the ultimate source. **Thenesko** means to die. So Jesus died in isolation. His death was unique, for he was virgin born and was the seed of the woman. He also had a unique death, in that he died spiritually for the sins of the world and then died physically so he could rise again. There was complete darkness around the cross when he bore the sins of the whole human race. He was isolated in his death. So **apothenesko** actually refers to Christ's spiritual death. Angels and humans were blacked out. He was totally alone. This means "his alone death." When the Bible says, "The wages of sin is death," this means spiritual death. Jesus became our substitute and said, "It is finished." Then he dismissed his spirit and died physically. Christ died twice in order that we might be born twice. **Apothenesko** is aorist, active, indicative. The aorist tense means the point of time when he died for our sins, the active voice means that he was the one who did the dying, and the indicative mood means the reality of his death. His death wasn't an illusion. It was a real, genuine, bona fide death. According to the scriptures the word is **huper** and it means "result." This means the Old Testament scriptures, starting with Genesis 3:15 and going through Isaiah 53:9. People were saved in Old Testament times just exactly as they are saved today. At death the soul went to a place called Paradise, in the heart of the earth. The Spirit went into the presence of God. His dead body was still on the cross but would soon be placed in a tomb. The Roman soldiers came up to Christ and saw he was already dead. They had seen him stand up under that ordeal. "As a lamb before his shearer is dumb, so he opened not his mouth," and the soldier plunged a sword into his side and out came blood and serum. After he died he still had blood in his body and he did not bleed to death. Now, in the Levitical offering, the lamb's throat was cut and the lamb bled to death. The guilty man placed his hand on the head of the animal, confessed his sins, and the lamb bleeding to death was a picture of the fact that the man's sins had been taken away. Leviticus, Chapter One, teaches this. It is a picture of the cross, but it pictures the spiritual death rather than the physical death of Christ. "The life of the flesh is in the blood" refers to animals only, not to men. In man the life is in the soul, not in the blood. So the blood refers to the spiritual death of Christ, not to his physical death. This is what is called a representative analogy. The animal's death is not an exact analogy, but a representative analogy. Every single animal sacrifice pointed to the cross.

1 Corinthians 15:4: "And that he was buried, and that he rose again the third day according to the scriptures." "And that he was buried" refers to the fact that he was placed in the tomb of Joseph of Arimathaea. His soul was in paradise and his spirit was in the presence of the Father. His body was in the grave, Luke 23:63. His soul was in paradise as in Luke 23:43 and Psalm 16:10. His spirit was in the presence of the Father as in Luke 23:46. For three days this was true, and then he arose. "He arose" is a perfect, passive, indicative. The perfect tense means he arose and would remain that way forever. The passive voice means that the Father and the Holy Spirit raised him from the grave. The indicative mood means the reality of the resurrection. God the Father sent the Holy Spirit and he brought the soul up from paradise. The soul and spirit were placed in a new body. He walked through the stone and he walked out of that grave and then appeared many times. God the Father and God the Holy Spirit cannot be destroyed. All of this is according to scripture, as in Isaiah 52:13 and 53:10.

Paul is here attempting to address the Greek mind and demonstrate that the resurrection is a part of the gospel. When you believe in Christ the emphasis is on the death of Christ, but then you move on to the resurrection and you can't separate the two. They are halves of the same whole. The moment you believe in Jesus you have an eternal existence and this means you will have a resurrection body exactly like that of the Son of God. This is a part of God's provision for you. He provides salvation and he also provides a resurrection body. Resurrection is an integral part of the gospel message.

THE FACT OF THE RESURRECTION

In our last study we surveyed the philosophical concept of death as taught by Plato and Socrates. According to the Greek translation, the body was regarded as something evil and they all looked forward to the day when the soul would leave the body. However, they couldn't accept the idea of reentering a human body even though it was a glorious resurrection body. Thus, the Corinthians refused to accept the idea of bodily resurrection because it was in direct conflict with their Greek philosophy and their Greek culture.

In our last study we saw that the resurrection is a vital part of the gospel and is in fact the capstone of it. In verses 5-20 of this chapter we have the account of a visible, actual, factual resurrection for all who believe in the Lord Jesus Christ. In other words, resurrection is a part of the plan of God.

Phase one of the plan of God is salvation. Christ died for us and we believe in him and he saves us. Then in phase two, which is the living of the Christian life, every believer is in full-time Christian service and is an ambassador and is a priest. Then at the point of physical death we move into phase three, and the resurrection is the means by which we enter it. The resurrection will occur at the point of physical death or at the rapture, whichever happens to come first. Genesis 1-11 is the story of the first dispensation, but at the end of this dispensation there was no resurrection, for Christ must set the pattern and he is the firstfruits. No one had a resurrection body until Christ had one, and up to now he is the only one who has been resurrected. (Please recall that the Bible gives many stories of bodies being resuscitated, but none resurrected up to this point. The story of the raising of Lazarus is a good scripture to study at this point. John 11:38-44.)

Once a person is resurrected, that person never dies again. 1 Corinthians 15:5: "This mortal must put on immortality." After the first dispensation, which is related in Genesis 1-11, we then move into the Dispensation of Israel which moves down to the cross, but the cross interrupted that dispensation and cut it short seven years. Please recall there was no resurrection in the Jewish dispensation. At the moment the Jewish age was interrupted, the Church Age began and in this age there can be resurrection, and will be, because Christ has already risen.

1 Thessalonians 4:16-17: "For the Lord himself shall descend from heaven with a shout, with the voice of the archangel, and with the trump of God: and the dead in Christ shall rise first: Then we which are alive and

remain shall be caught up together with them in the clouds to meet the Lord in the air: and so shall we ever be with the Lord." The dead "in Christ" refers to Church Age believers only, not Old Testament saints. Once the tribulation is over, then there will be the resurrection of Old Testament saints and tribulation martyrs. At that time all living saints will move into the Millennium and at the end of the Millennium there will be a final resurrection of all Millennial saints who will at that time get a resurrection body.

So we have four parts to the first resurrection.

The First Resurrection

1. Christ the firstfruits. 1 Cor. 15:23.
2. The Church Age saints, dead and living. 1 Thess. 4:16-17.
3. Then all Old Testament saints will be raised at the end of the tribulation. 1 Cor. 15:23.
4. Finally at the end of the Millennium all the Millennial saints will be raised up. Rev. 11:18b.

Revelation 20:6: "Blessed and holy is he that hath part in the first resurrection: on such the second death hath no power, but they shall be priests of God and of Christ, and shall reign with him a thousand years." But you see, you can't teach this to the Greeks, the Corinthians, for they won't even admit that there is going to be a resurrection.

1 Corinthians 15:5: "And that he was seen of Cephas, then of the twelve." How can Paul prove to a Greek audience that the resurrection occurred? How can they be sure that Christ actually arose from the dead? Well, one good way is by calling on witnesses who saw him after his resurrection. People actually saw him after he arose. So in this verse Paul reminds the Corinthians that the resurrected Christ was seen by Cephas and then by the twelve. The first thing Christ did when he arose was to go to Tartarus so he could explain to the fallen ones why they were being sentenced to the lake of fire. The first resurrection appearance was not top side, but was under the earth in Tartarus. Then Christ returned to the earth and came out of the tomb. Then angels came and rolled the stone away to call attention to the fact that Christ had already gone from the grave. The stone was rolled away not to let Christ out but to let the world in so they could observe the resurrection. After the tomb was empty, there were about 18 resurrection appearances.

So Paul was saying to the Corinthians, "So you Greeks don't believe in a resurrection? Then let us call on some witnesses."

Cephas was the third one to whom he appeared.

He first appeared to Mary Magdalene. John 20:16; Mark 16:9.

His next appearance was to the other women. Matthew 28:9.

His third appearance was to Cephas. (Our passage here — 1 Corinthians 15:5.) The Corinthians knew Simon Peter, and they would be likely to accept his witness.

68

His fourth appearance was to two disciples on the Road to Emmaus, Cleopas and another. Mark 16:12; Luke 24:13-31.

His fifth appearance was to the disciples in the upper room. John 20:19-20.

His sixth appearance was to the disciples plus Thomas. John 20:24-29.

His seventh appearance was to the disciples on the Sea of Galilee. John 21:1.

His eighth appearance was to the apostle Paul. Acts 9:3-6

His ninth appearance was to James. 1 Corinthians 15:7.

He appeared again to the disciples with a specific commission. Luke 24:44-49; Acts 1:3-8.

And his last appearance was on the Mt. of Olives. Luke 24:50-53; Acts 1:9-12.

1 Corinthians 15:6: "After that, he was seen of above five hundred brethren at once; of whom the greater part remain unto this present, but some are fallen asleep." "He was seen" is an aorist, passive, indicative of **horao.** They saw him clearly. Many of those 500 were still alive when Paul wrote this to the Corinthians. In fact, the majority of them were still alive. Some had died. (The resurrection of Jesus took place in 30 A.D. and Paul was writing this to the Corinthians in 57 A.D.) So 27 years after it happened the majority of those who saw Jesus after his resurrection were still alive.

The word for fallen asleep here is **koimao** and it means to be asleep in anticipation of waking up again, which is the resurrection. This is a technical word used of believers only. Paul here was striking at their neo-platonism and their rationalism. Paul is saying, "One day you Corinthians will also be asleep and will wake up in the resurrection." When sleep appears in the Bible it refers to the body only and not to the soul and spirit.

1 Corinthians 15:7: "After that, he was seen of James; then of all the apostles." This is James, the Lord's stepbrother. After the virgin birth of Jesus, Joseph and Mary had a family.

Matthew 13:55: "Is not this the carpenter's son? is not his mother called Mary? and his brethren, James, and Joseph, Jr., and Simon, and Judas?" James was the oldest, next to Jesus. He wrote the book of **James** and was the pastor of the Jerusalem church. Then there was Joseph, Jr. and Simon and Judas and several daughters. James was skeptical and would not accept the hypostatic union of Christ until he saw him in his resurrection body.

Acts 1:14: "These all continued with one accord in prayer and supplication, with the women, and Mary the mother of Jesus, and with his brethren."

Galatians 1:19: "But other of the apostles saw I none, save James the Lord's brother." James had a hard-headed practical mind and was never really convinced that Jesus was the Son of God until he saw him in his resurrection body. So James might be classified as a hostile witness. Then Christ was seen by all the disciples on a mountain in Galilee.

1 Corinthians 15:8: "And last of all he was seen of me also, as of one born out of due time." This may be the most interesting appearance of all. Paul became the replacement for Judas. The church held an election in Acts 1, but it was an ill-advised procedure, since Matthias was never intended to be the one to replace Judas. In fact, you never hear his name mentioned again in the record. The Lord chose Paul to replace Judas, and this is recorded in **1 Corinthians** 12. The disciples made a beautiful prayer about Matthias and said, "Whom thou hast chosen," but the Lord hadn't chosen him at all. So the slot was open and Paul moved in and became the right replacement for Judas. And Christ didn't appear to Paul just once but several times. You see, in order to be an apostle one had to have seen the risen Christ.

Paul saw him on the road to Damascus, according to Acts 9. Then Paul saw him an Arabian in the desert. (Galatians 1:13.) Christ appeared to him again in the prison. (Acts 23:11.) Then Christ appeared to him again in the temple. (Acts 22.) Paul refers to his apostleship "as one born out of due time." It is an idiom used for abortion. It is very suitable for Paul for at the time of the actual resurrection Paul was still unsaved. (1 Timothy 1:12-15.) This scripture tells us that Paul was the worst sinner that ever lived. Think of all the Russian and Chinese Communists and all the gangsters and criminals — to say that Paul was the worst sinner that ever lived you are really saying something.

The greatest person that ever lived was a Jew named Jesus Christ, and the worst person that ever lived was a Jew named Saul of Tarsus and of the Tribe of Benjamin. So the best and worst were from the Southern Kingdom. Paul was a very moral man, a very righteous man; he was a Pharisee and a law keeper. He had made more points with God under the Ten Commandments that you could ever add up. He was the most religious person that ever lived and the most legalistic. He killed the imprisoned in the name of religion. Jesus had the most grace. Paul had the most legalism. He was born again out of due time, but not born too late.

Paul is now going to describe for us how he came from the worst sinner to the greatest believer. He became a maximum grace man. You remember he committed one act of legalism, and as a result he got four years of discipline from God. Paul should have kept going west, but he had a passion for those Jerusalem Jews, and he turned and went east and got out of the geographical will of God.

1 Corinthians 15:9: "For I am the least of the apostles, that am not meet to be called an apostle, because I persecuted the church of God." Paul says that he was the least of the apostles. He didn't get to walk with Jesus three years, didn't see the miracles, and he wasn't there when the Church Age was

launched. Paul here confessed that he wasn't fit to be an apostle for he kept on persecuting the church.

1 Corinthians 15:10: "But by the grace of God I am what I am: and his grace which was bestowed upon me was not in vain; but I laboured more abundantly than they all: yet not I, but the grace of God which was with me." Here is the secret of Paul. "By the grace of God," Paul says, "I am what I am." Grace is an instrument that can convert the worst into the best. Literally these words say, "I am what I have become." The first "I am" is from **eimi** but the second "I am" is from **ginomai. Ginomai** means to become something that you were not before. "In vain" means useless, empty. Please remember that every believer has the same chance at the grace of God. God has made the provision. After Paul was converted he went to Arabia to learn doctrine, and he never stopped learning while his ministry was based on grace. Well, how did it turn out?

Philippians 4:11: "Not that I speak in respect of want: for I have learned, in whatsoever state I am, therewith to be content."

Paul says here that he had learned how to have inner contentment. Notice Paul says, "I know." His contentment was based on his knowledge of Bible doctrine. The "I am instructed" is a perfect tense and it means his learning is permanent and abiding.

Back in 1 Corinthians 15:10 Paul says, "His grace upon me," and he means it is always there. Knowledge of doctrine leads to orientation to grace. But remember this — grace can't operate in your life if you are unacquainted with doctrine. If you do not operate on grace, then you operate on legalism. Paul said, "I laboured" and it is from **kopiao** and it means to labor to the point of exhaustion.

Knowledge of doctrine plus the filling of the Holy Spirit equals the production of divine good. Divine good is always a grace production. So Paul here is basing his argument for the resurrection on the fact that many witnessed the resurrected Christ. But he is going to move on from this argument into the greatest argument about the resurrection that we find in all literature, as in the next verses he proves beyond a shadow of a doubt that Christ arose from the grave.

71

THE BIBLE'S MOST PROFOUND LOGIC
CONCERNING THE RESURRECTION

Keep in mind as we make this study that the Greeks did not believe in a bodily resurrection. Taking their ideas from the teachings of Plato and Socrates they regarded the physical body as evil. To the Greeks the soul was the important thing. They all looked forward to the day when after death the soul would be liberated from the body. The idea of receiving a resurrection body after death was totally repugnant to them, so they totally rejected the idea of a resurrection body. Here Paul presents the resurrection as an essential part of the gospel. Now this doesn't mean that you have to believe in the resurrection in order to be saved. All you have to know in order to be saved is that Christ died for you and that you are willing to accept the provisions he has made for your sins on the cross. It doesn't take much faith to be saved, in fact, hardly any faith at all. The Bible says that if we have the faith of a little mustard seed, we can be saved.

1 Corinthians 15:11: "Therefore whether it were I or they, so we preach and so ye believed." Paul had explained to the Corinthians that they should believe in the resurrection and to strengthen his argument he quoted witnesses who had actually seen the resurrected Christ. These witnesses included Paul himself. The first century preachers had a great deal to say about the resurrection, and Paul was one of those preachers.

In this verse Paul said, "Therefore whether I or they." So Paul had taught the resurrection, and the other apostles had also taught the resurrection. The resurrection repercussions are quite obvious from two viewpoints. From the standpoint of the Lord Jesus Christ we have **Hebrews 1:13:** "But to which of the angels said he at any time, Sit on my right hand, until I make thine enemies thy footstool?" Then from the standpoint of the believer we have **Philippians 3:21**: "Who shall change our vile body, that it may be fashioned like unto his glorious body, according to the working whereby he is able even to subdue all things unto himself." We believers are going to have a resurrection body exactly like Christ's. So no matter what doctrine you use, the doctrine of the angelic conflict, or the doctrine of the believer's eternal future, the resurrection is essential. The resurrection is the link between Christ on earth and his being seated at the right hand of God, at which point the conquest of his enemies begins. Paul then said, "So we keep on preaching the resurrection." They all knew that the resurrection of Christ was a solid fact and that is why they kept on preaching it. The apostles knew it was a fact, and Paul knew it was a fact. Paul saw the resurrected Christ on four different occasions; therefore, he had ample evidence on which to base his preaching.

The word "preach" is in the present tense, and this means that he just kept on preaching this great truth. In the next phrase, "And so ye believed," the word "believed" is in the aorist tense and refers to the moment they put their faith in Christ. So it actually means that in a point of time one believes and that lasts forever. You can't reaffirm your faith if by reaffirmation you mean you have to be saved over again. Once saved, you are always saved and the aorist tense here proves this. Someone may tell you that at the point of your salvation, you didn't know what you were doing and now you need to do it all over again and accept him as Lord. But that isn't necessarily true. You need to accept him as Lord but that is not a part of the salvation package. It is rather a part of the edification of the soul, and this comes about by learning doctrine and by applying doctrine to your daily living. If someone tells you that if you don't remember the date and the hour and the real feeling you had when you were saved, that you were not saved at all, you just discount what they say to you. You are saved the second you believe in Christ, and whether you can recall all about it, what you said and how you felt, has nothing at all to do with the reality of your experience. Your being saved doesn't depend on your memory or your feeling, but on the power of Jesus Christ to save you when you trusted him. So here in these next verses we have the fact of the resurrection based on logic. This is one of the greatest pieces of logic found in the Word of God.

1 Corinthians 15:12: "Now if Christ be preached that he rose from the dead, how say some among you that there is no resurrection of the dead?" In dealing with the Greeks, who had denied the resurrection because it contradicted their background, Paul uses logic to show them how wrong they are. Now we all have things in our background which disagree with true doctrine. Which are we going to accept, the authority of the Word of God or the prejudice which comes from our background? The Greeks habitually thought in terms of no bodily resurrection. Having a resurrection body was to the Greek mind an impossibility. It was a terrible thing. Now they believed in eternal life, which meant that after death they would have a free soul and live in happiness and contentment forever. All of this was compatible with all they had learned from Plato and Socrates. So they had had over 400 years of background prejudice concerning a resurrection body and were therefore determined they were not going to believe in a resurrection body.

Now what can you do with people like that? Paul is going to do something in this passage that shocked his listeners. He is going, for the sake of argument, to assume that the resurrection didn't take place. So Paul here employed logic and a debater's technique to show them how the resurrection is an established fact.

The "if" in this verse is a true first class condition and it means "if" and it is true. Then there is a debater's first class condition, and that is to assume something is not true, just for argument's sake, in order to prove that it is true. Paul was a genius in debater's technique.

"If Christ be preached that he rose from the dead, how say some among you there is no resurrection?" This "you" refers to Corinthian Christians so this shows that one can be a Christian and not accept the teaching of the resurrection because it has not been properly taught. Many are saved who do not understand the doctrine of the resurrection.

1 Corinthians 15:13: "But if there be no resurrection of the dead, then is Christ not risen." Here in this verse Paul uses a debater's first class condition. He is going to assume something is not true in order to prove that it is true. He assumes something is true in order to refute it. So Paul here denies there was a resurrection in order to prove that it occurred. Now as soon as you assume that something does not exist, your mind often begins to say to you that it does. So for argument's sake, Paul denies the resurrection. So it is possible to deny something just to find out how real that something is.

In substance, Paul is saying to the Corinthians something like this, "Say, you Corinthians, let's assume for the time being that the resurrection is not true, then if it is not, what would be the results of no resurrection?" Then Paul will move on to show them that they really can't live without the resurrection. (Illustration — suppose you love a person very much, but you fall out with that person to the extent that you say, "I'll wipe that person out of my mind to the extent that he doesn't even exist." But every time you hear the music you heard with that person, you are driven to think of her. And there are a thousand little details that come to mind that cause you to think of that person. So you discover by vowing that you do not love that person, just how much you really do.)

"Then" introduces a logical conclusion. If there be no resurrection, then Christ was not risen. This would imply that those who believed they had seen a resurrected Christ were living under an optical illusion. But even if one person had had an optical illusion, it is scarcely possible that so many witnesses could have had an optical illusion about the same person. All the apostles saw the resurrected Christ, and 500 saw him at one time on a mountain in Galilee. Is it possible that all these people could have had an optical illusion at the same time? Well, you can't say that Paul and the Apostles and the 500 were all liars, can you? Yet this is exactly what you must say if you say that there was no resurrection, and in substance, this is what the Corinthians were saying when they said that there was no resurrection.

So Paul is saying to the Corinthians, "If there is no resurrection, then I am a liar and the apostles are liars and those 500 others are also liars." The Corinthians knew that Paul and Peter and all those Christians were not liars.

And today we know the same thing. Peter and Paul and those 500 were not living under an optical illusion, and they were not lying. They had actually seen the living, resurrected Christ, and they all knew it.

1 Corinthians 15:14: "And if Christ be not risen, then is our preaching vain, and your faith is also vain." This "if" is another debater's first class condition, assuming that something is not true in order to prove that it is. The logical conclusion of this assumption is that their preaching was in vain. **Kenos** is the word for vain. The word **metaia** is going to be used later on for vain, but one word refers to the person, and the other word refers to the content of the message. **Kenos** refers to the content, and means that the content is void. If Christ be not risen, then their preaching is void of content, it is useless, it is empty. It leads people up a blind alley. It is a "no exit" street. Then Paul says that also this would make your faith useless. In other words, without the resurrection, your salvation package is not complete. Christ was not resurrected as a part of the salvation package, but Christ was resurrected because of salvation and as a logical result of it. **Dia** plus the accusative means "because of."

Turn to Romans 4:24: "But for us also, to whom it shall be imputed, if we believe on him that raised up Jesus our Lord from the dead." The "if we believe" here is "because we believe."

Romans 4:25: "Who was delivered for our offenses, and was raised again for our justification." It should read, "Who was delivered to the cross **because** of our offenses and was raised **because** of our justification." He was raised because he had already justified us on the cross. Jesus was raised from the grave **"because"** salvation was completed on the cross. He was not raised **for** the completion of salvation, but **because** of the completion of salvation. Resurrection was the perfect logical conclusion of the perfect salvation that was completed on the cross. The resurrection does not complete salvation. When Christ said, "Finished," salvation was completed. The resurrection simply signifies that salvation had been completed on the cross. The resurrection began a new phase of the angelic conflict. Salvation demands a phase three, which is life after death, which is resurrection.

So Paul's debater's technique goes something like this, "Since there is no resurrection, Christ did not rise, and since Christ did not rise, your faith is useless and faith is also incomplete."

1 Corinthians 15:15: "Yea, and we are found false witnesses of God; because we have testified of God that he raised up Christ: whom he raised not up, if so be that the dead rise not." Paul now says that if there is no resurrection all these preachers have been proclaiming a lie. "We are found false witnesses **concerning God.**" God is perfect and he will not be represented by someone who is lying about him. At this point, the Greek minds

were really working, and they were beginning to see how stupid they had been by glibly saying, "There is no resurrection." The word used here for "God" is singular, but it is used for God the Father, and God the Holy Spirit.

Psalm 16:10: "For thou wilt not leave my soul in hell; neither wilt thou suffer thine Holy One to see corruption."

Acts 2:31-32: "He seeing this before spake of the resurrection of Christ, that his soul was not left in hell, neither his flesh did see corruption. This Jesus hath God raised up, whereof we all are witnesses."

1 Thessalonians 1:10: "And to wait for his Son from heaven, whom he raised from the dead, even Jesus, which delivered us from the wrath to come."

The Holy Spirit also had a part in the resurrection.

Romans 8:11: "But if the Spirit of him that raised up Jesus from the dead dwell in you, he that raised up Christ from the dead shall also quicken your mortal bodies by his Spirit that dwelleth in you."

1 Peter 3:13: "For Christ also hath once suffered for sins, the just for the unjust, that he might bring us to God, being put to death in the flesh, but quickened by the Spirit."

Now if God the Father raised Christ from the dead, why does it say that God the Holy Spirit raised him from the dead? Is there a conflict here in scripture? No, there is no conflict. When Christ died his human spirit went to be with the Father. His soul went into paradise. His body went into the grave. So the Father sent his human spirit back into his body and the Holy Spirit brought his soul from paradise and his soul reentered his body and immediately Christ went and made his victorious announcement to the spirits in prison. So Paul says here that if there is no resurrection, then are the dead not raised.

1 Corinthians 15:16: "For if the dead rise not, then is not Christ raised." Here is another debater's first class condition with the use of "if." He is assuming for argument's sake that this is not true. Here is a repetition of verse 13. So we have three assumptions —

1. Our preaching is vain.
2. Your faith is vain.
3. We are all liars.

Now we have to return to the premise and start over again because those Greeks were thinking about these three statements Paul had just made, and he had to jerk their minds back to the original truth.

1 Corinthians 15:17: "And if Christ be not raised, your faith is vain, ye are yet in your sins." Now Paul uses the first class condition again, and for the words "Your faith is vain" this time he uses the word **metaia** and not **kenos. Mataios** means void of truth. **Kenos** means void of quality, content is useless.

77

So Paul is saying something like this, "If you are believing in someone who is still in the grave, dead, there is no future, there is no eternal life." The logical conclusion is this, "You are yet in your sins, you are unsaved. If you do not believe in life beyond the grave, you are unsaved. You have accepted a false doctrine."

In other words, your faith is a lie, and because your faith is a lie, the object of your faith cannot save you and you do not have a resurrection body which will withstand the destruction of the universe. According to 2 Peter 3:10, the earth will be destroyed by a great nuclear explosion. The resurrection body will withstand the greatest exposion of all time, and we will live in a resurrection body in a new heaven and a new earth.

1 Corinthians 15:18: "Then they also which are fallen asleep in Christ are perished." Now Paul gives another logical conclusion: If there be no resurrection, then those who have fallen asleep in Christ are perished. All those Corinthian Christians had loved ones who were dead. The words for "fallen asleep" come from **koimao** and mean to sleep with the anticipation of waking up. So this word is not used simply for falling asleep, but for Christian death. Falling asleep contains "waking up" in it. The aorist tense refers to the moment of physical death. The passive voice means we receive death, for if it were active voice it would mean that we would all commit suicide. And the indicative mood means the reality of death for everyone.

We will see each other in our resurrection bodies, and at that time, we will have no old sin natures and will commit no acts of human good. We will know each other and live together forever in this perfect state. The expression "therefore they also which have received sleep" is used in 1 Corinthians 11:30, and there it refers to the sin unto death. 1 Thessalonians 4:14 uses the same expression and means sleeping with the idea of waking up. Remember, the soul and the spirit do not sleep. **Koimao** refers to the body's waking up. When the body dies everything that is living within has to leave, so the soul and the spirit depart. This is one time when every Christian is going to wake up "on the right side of the bed" as we say. We will wake up under ideal circumstances. This is a beautiful phrase to emphasize the waking up of the body. We receive life from God, and listen carefully, WE HAVE NO RIGHT TO TAKE OUR OWN LIVES. It won't send a believer to hell to commit suicide, but it is an act of disobedience for anyone to take his own life. The action of the participle precedes the action of the main verb, and the main verb here is "are perished."

1 Corinthians 15:19: "If in this life only we have hope in Christ, we are of all men most miserable." "If in this life only we have hope in Christ," and for the sake of debate Paul assumes this to be true. No resurrection means there is no hope beyond this life.

And the conclusion of it all is that we are most miserable. When you reject any point of doctrine, it always leads to personal misery. You can't keep misery out when you don't have Bible doctrine filling your mind.

XIII

THE PROFOUND RESURRECTION ASSUMPTION

This passage looks at the resurrection from the standpoint of historical fact.

1 Corinthians 15:20: "But now is Christ risen from the dead, and become the firstfruits of them that slept." "But now is Christ risen." That word for risen is a perfect tense, and it means that it is an established fact forever. There is a time when the Millennium will be over and God will have pulled together all the loose ends of the angelic conflict. The purposes of the creation of man will be fulfilled, and at that time this old earth is going to be destroyed. Isaiah speaks about it, Peter speaks about it, and John in Revelation speaks about the destruction that will come to this present universe. It will be a tremendous nuclear explosion, and the entire universe will be destroyed.

2 Peter 3:10: "But the day of the Lord will come as a thief in the night; in the which the heavens shall pass away with a great noise, and the elements shall melt with fervent heat, the earth also and the works that are therein shall be burned up." When this destruction comes there will be no place to hide, and there will be no system of defense. There will be no cave or hole to which one can go for safety. But there is a refuge. Over in the Book of Hebrews we are told that the resurrection body will withstand this explosion. Nothing can touch or harm or destroy the resurrected body of a believer. The resurrected believer has an adequate place of protection, a perfect air raid shelter. The resurrection body is that perfect protection.

The word "risen" is in the passive voice and means that Christ received resurrection. Jesus Christ is the first person to receive resurrection, and up to this time, he is the only person who has ever been resurrected. "Risen" is in the indicative mood and this means the reality of the resurrected Christ. The Feast of the Firstfruits is in view at this particular point (Leviticus 23:9-14). This is one of those types of feasts that always worried the Jews. They always had a clear idea, generally, about their feasts. The Passover pictured the Messiah dying for their sins. We read, "Christ our passover is sacrificed for us." Immediately following the Passover began the Feast of the Unleavened Bread, and this feast lasted for eight days. The Jews also had a Feast called Pentecost and they understood that feast also. But right in the middle of the Feast of the Passover, they had a feast called **"Firstfruits,"** and it always occurred on Sunday, the first day of the week. (Of course, they regarded Sunday very much like we regard Monday in our week.) Then 50 days later, always on Sunday, the Feast of Pentecost began which marked the beginning of the fifth cycle of discipline for Israel. Then we have a six-month gap until the Feast of the Trumpets, which speaks of the return of Christ to the earth and the regathering of Israel. The Feast of Atonement speaks of the fact that only born-again individuals will go into the Millennium. Then comes the Feast of Tabernacle, which speaks of the Millennial reign of the Lord Jesus Christ. So only two feasts really bothered the Jews and both of those feasts began on Sunday; Pentecost and the Firstfruits. The Firstfruits especially bothered the Jews, for they had a hard time accepting the resurrection. The Pharisees believed in the resurrection but the Sadducees didn't. The Herodians scarcely had an opinion about the issue. And as Hellenistic culture came in, the idea of resurrection fell under attack. So the Feast of the Firstfruits was not a very happy feast for the Jews.

"But now is Christ risen from the dead and has **become.**" The word, "become" is **ginomai** and it means to become something that you were not before. In his resurrection Christ had become the pattern for every born-again man in all the earth. This feast involved animal sacrifice. Keep in mind that animal sacrifice laid emphasis on the work of Christ, on the cross, and food offerings laid emphasis on the person of Christ. You see, the righteousness and justice of God means that Christ can't have any contact with the human race. But the cross satisfied the righteousness and justice of God, and following the cross, God was free to save man and have eternal fellowship with him. The love of God therefore is free to operate in our behalf in all three phases of our existence.

In Phase One, which is our salvation, God was free to love man because of the cross.

In Phase Two, which is our Christian living day by day, God loves man in spite of his failure.

In Phase Three, which is eternity, God will love us forever. But the Jews didn't like to relate propitiation to resurrection. The waving of the sheaf of grain before the Lord was their way of saying, in substance, "I know that God will provide for his own." Now they understood their own economy, and they knew God would provide for their needs. But what they didn't like to admit was that this feast of the Firstfruits related propitiation to resurrection. Jesus came out of the grave in resurrection because propitiation was an accomplished fact. The resurrection is a guarantee that propitiation may apply to any member of the human race, when that member places his faith in Jesus Christ. The resurrection is our guarantee of this perfect future with God throughout eternity. The waving of the grain was a guarantee of the coming harvest. The resurrection of Jesus Christ was a guarantee that every believer in the whole human race will spend all eternity in a perfect resurrection body.

The resurrection body is a perfect bomb shelter and it will survive the destruction of the heavens and the earth. So Christ's resurrection is called the Firstfruits. The resurrection is a key to the future. It is a guarantee and is a link between God seated in heaven and the work of Christ on the cross. He bore our sins in his humanity. So it was the humanity of Christ that was resurrected and it will be our humanity that will be resurrected. The resurrection of Christ is the half-way house between the cross and the angelic conflict. When Christ went to the cross, his humanity was inferior to angels. We read in Hebrews that he was made a little lower than the angels. When in a resurrection body he ascended to the right hand of the Father, his resurrected humanity was demonstrated to be superior to angels.

Hebrews 1:13-14: "But to which of the angels said he at any time, Sit my right hand, until I make thine enemies thy footstool? Are they not all ministering spirits, sent forth to minister for them who shall be heirs of salvation?" At salvation we pass the point of propitiation, and we enter into union with Christ and positionally become superior to angelic creatures. The enemies of all this are the fallen angels under the leadership of Satan, and they are going to be made Christ's footstool.

So now we enter into his glory, and his resurrection is our guarantee of this fact. Deity is not subject to resurrection. Deity was present but deity couldn't be resurrected, for deity was already alive. Deity can't be nailed to a cross, for you can't confine deity by nails to a cross. So it is the resurrected humanity of Christ that is our guarantee that our humanity has a future. Our physical bodies as they are now constituted can't withstand a nuclear blast, but our resurrection bodies will not be affected at all by such a catastrophe. Now, in this world, our physical bodies are subject to all kinds of disease. The minute we are born our bodies begin to deteriorate, and sooner or later we will die physically. Paul tells us what physical death is like. He died once under a pile of rocks and was caught up into the third heaven and in that experience he learned a great deal. It was a great ecstatic experience for him.

(Illustration: I saw my own father die at the age of 84 and I saw excitement on my father's face. He was as excited about meeting God as a little child is excited about getting to the Christmas tree on Christmas morning. Happiness was dancing in his eyes, and God's great presence filled the room as his spirit went to God.)

So remember this — we believers are going to have a first class resurrection body and nothing can dent it or touch it or destroy it.

Philippians 3:21: "Who shall change our vile body, that it may be fashioned like unto his glorious body, according to the working whereby he is able even to subdue all things unto himself." In our resurrection bodies we won't even have to exercise every day, and this fact reminds me that I now live in a body of corruption. (Now I know some of my friends already think they are in resurrection bodies for they quit exercising a long time ago. Of course, they will find out better a little later on.)

In the resurrection we are going to have a body that is glorious. You can eat or not eat for eating will be optional. You can sleep or not sleep, breathe or not breathe. Sometimes when we get sick and our bodies pain us, we are tempted to be like the Greeks and say that we don't want to have a resurrection body. But remember, in the resurrection body, there will be no sickness, no pain, no disease. Doctors will be out of a job in God's eternal kingdom. Now how do I know this? Well, I've been handed a guarantee and so have you, and that guarantee is the resurrected body of Jesus Christ.

The fact of Christ's resurrection signifies the fact that you and I are in full-time Christian service. Possibly you may say to yourself that you don't feel like you are in full-time Christian service. But indeed you are. You are, and all you do is to be done as unto the Lord. Once Christ was raised from the dead and ascended and was seated at God's right hand, he had to have representatives on the earth, and we are those representatives. Once Christ is seated in heaven it means he cannot be here in person, and he places his spirit in us so we can represent him. The moment the humanity of Christ sat down in his resurrection body, every Christian was given the indwelling Holy Spirit; every believer was placed in full-time Christian service; and every believer became a priest. Once the veil of the temple was rent in twain, this fact made it possible for the most humble believer to go in and transact business with God. After Christ arose from the dead the priest waved the grain, a guarantee of the harvest, but he didn't go on to the proper conclusion, realizing that this meant that since Christ was resurrected, this is our guarantee of a resurrection.

This verse says, "of them that slept" and the word for sleep is **koimao** and it means to go to sleep with the idea of waking up. There is no such thing as soul or spirit sleeping. Your physical body goes to sleep, once the soul and spirit leave it. (It may be that we spend too much on the burial of dead bodies. We bring soldiers back clear across the world and spend millions of dollars on the burial of their physical bodies.) It really doesn't matter too much how or where your physical body is buried. The real you is your soul and spirit and the soul and spirit leave the body at the moment of physical death. At the moment of the resurrection the soul and the spirit return to that sacred dust which reenters the physical body in the resurrection.

1 Corinthians 15:21: "For since by man came death, by man came also the resurrection of the dead." Now we have some contrasts. Here we have **dia** plus the genitive and it means "Through the instrumentality of a man came death." This means Adam died spiritually. God said to Adam in

84

Genesis, "Dying, thou shalt die." That first dying was spiritual death. Over 900 years later Adam died physically. Spiritual death is overcome at the cross. Physical death is overcome by the resurrection. Propitiation guarantees overcoming spiritual death by having faith in Christ. Physical death is overcome by the guarantee of the resurrection. When we believe in Christ we have overcome spiritual death. This truth is also brought out in verse 26 and in Romans 8:1: "There is no judgment to them that are in Christ Jesus." So we have two guarantees:

1. Faith in Christ guarantees everlasting life.
2. The resurrection guarantees that the physical resurrected body will live forever and be as perfect as Christ's.

1 Corinthians 15:22: "For as in Adam all die, even so in Christ shall all be made alive." "In Adam all die," please notice here that physical death and spiritual death are never linked. When Adam sinned he died immediately. He died spiritually, and it was 900 years before he died physically. We are born spiritually dead, and Adam became spiritually dead by an act of volitional disobedience. So God handles spiritual death by the cross, and he handles physical death by the resurrection.

Please notice it says, "Even so in Christ shall all be made alive" and this means that the potential for eternal life is always there, available to all who believe. This "shall all be made alive" is in the future tense, passive voice. At any future moment when one believes, he is made alive by the power and promise of Almighty God.

1 Corinthians 15:23: "But every man in his own order: Christ the firstfruits; afterward they that are Christ's at his coming." So we read, "every man in his own battalion." Here is the reviewing stand and God watches them as they go by.

Company A — Christ passes by first. He is the "Firstfruits."

Company B — These are the Church Age Saints.

Company C — These are the Old Testament Saints and the Tribulation Martyrs.

Company D — These are the Millennial Saints.

Every man in his own order, his own rank, his own battalion. And this is called "The First Resurrection." It will take place over thousands of years, in the order listed above.

Then comes the Second Resurrection which is for all **unbelievers,** and they will be judged and cast into the lake of fire. Look at some of the scripture for this order.

Company A — Christ. 1 Cor. 15:23, Romans 1:4, 1 Thess. 1:10.

Company B — The Church Saints. 1 Thess. 4:16-18.

Company C — Old Testament Saints. Daniel 12:13, Isaiah 26:19-20, Revelation 20:4, Matthew 21:24-31.

Company D — Millennial Saints. The Second Resurrection. Revelation 20:12-15.

1 Corinthians 15:24: "Then cometh the end, when he shall have delivered up the kingdom of God, even the Father; when he shall have put down all rule and all authority and power." This is the last phase of Christ's first conquest of his enemies. Then cometh the end. Jesus is going to deliver up the Kingdom of God, even the Father.

He has put down all rule and authority and power. Satan is involved in the rule, and he is put down. Satan has delegated authority to fallen angels and to fallen man, and this authority will be put down. Power refers to demon power and all demons will be removed from the earth in the Millennium.

Zechariah 13:2: "And it shall come to pass in that day, saith the Lord of hosts, that I will cut off the names of the idols out of the land, and they shall no more be remembered: and also I will cause the prophets and the unclean spirit to pass out of the land."

Colossians 2:15: "And having spoiled principalities and powers, he made a shew of them openly, triumphing over them in it."

1 Corinthians 15:25: "For he must reign, till he hath put all enemies under his feet." This is the Millennial reign of Christ. In our next study we will look at the results of the resurrection.

 **XIV**

THE RESULTS OF THE RESURRECTION

As I have indicated in the previous chapters, the Greeks didn't believe in the resurrection, and they didn't want to have anything to do with a resurrection body. Following the teachings of Plato and Aristotle, they accepted the idea of a "free soul" that would exist throughout eternity, but they denied that there would be a resurrection body. Since the Greeks had completely rejected the possibility of a bodily resurrection, Paul attempts to correct their false concepts in the following passage.

1 Corinthians 15:26: "The last enemy that shall be destroyed is death." The whole concept of the plan of God in relation to mankind is to destroy the enemies of man one by one. The first enemies of man emerged as a result of the angelic conflict. Satan and all the demons are the enemies of man. This is stated in Hebrews 1:13 when God commanded Christ to sit on his right hand until his enemies were made into his footstool. The enemies referred to here are Satan and the demons. The other fundamental enemy to be defeated is the old sin nature. The old sin nature has an area of weakness, and from this area of weakness come sins. But the old sin nature also has an area of strength, and from this area arise human good and all human good is the enemy of man. Demonism is the enemy of man. But the last and final enemy is death. The word translated "destroy" here doesn't mean destroy, but it means to neutralize. It is from **katargeo**, two words, **kata** and **argeo**. **Argeo** means to be useless, and **kata** refers to a norm or standard. So this word means to neutralize something by a norm or standard, and here it means to neutralize death by the norm or standard of the plan of God. The plan of God pulls the stinger out of death. The verb in question is in the present tense and is a dramatic present. It is also passive voice, and this means that death receives this neutralization from God. The indicative mood refers to the reality of this neutralization. Now death cannot be neutralized without the actual bodily resurrection. Neo-Platonism said, "No resurrection body," but Christ appeared and rose again in order to neutralize all such teaching. However, the most startling fact to notice is that the neutralization of death is performed by two resurrections, which must now be elaborated.

The First Resurrection

1. Christ the firstfruits.
2. At the end of the Church Age, all Church Age saints are resurrected, both dead and living.
3. At the time of the Second Advent of Christ, all Old Testament saints and tribulational martyrs are raised up.

4. Millennial saints are raised up at the end of the Millennium.

So death is neutralized when all born-again people get a resurrection body.

The Second Resurrection

This resurrection is for unbelievers only and at this resurrection all of these are taken to the lake of fire. This will last for all eternity.

In spite of this truth, the Greeks said that the human soul was the only thing that went beyond the grave. So the Greeks actually believed in universal salvation. All you had to do to be saved was to be a member of the human race, and when you died your soul would go to the **Elysian Fields.** But the Word of God says something different. Death is neutralized, but death is really just the beginning of eternity. Death for the believer means happiness, perfection, eternity with the Lord. For the unbeliever death means hell, suffering, and separation from God.

1 Corinthians 15:27-28: "For he hath put all things under his feet. But when he saith all things are put under him, it is manifest that he is expected, which did put all things under him. And when all things shall be subdued unto him, then shall the Son also himself be subject unto him that put all things under him, that God may be all in all." One of the results of the resurrection is the triumph of God. Since God is perfect his plan is perfect. He plans for us in time and he plans for us in eternity. "Put all things" is from **hupotasso. Hupo** means authority or under, and **tasso** means rank. Everything is subordinated to an over-all objective. God has over-all objectives, and they are perfect. In eternity past God existed alone. But in the eternity of the future God will have the elect angels and all born-again believers of all time with him. God has a perfect plan that will allow all of these to live with him in perfection forever. In the interim, God has made provision for every man and every need of man. No problem is too great for the plan of God. And since God meets every need down here, he will also meet every need in eternity.

To enjoy the provision God has made for us in eternity, the soul is going to be in a body. When the soul is out of the body that person's soul is in a state of perfect ecstatics. Here our body is attached to a certain amount of pain. When something goes wrong in the body a nerve uses pain to send a message to the brain to tell us something is wrong. Now the human body isn't designed to fly out into space. We have learned to fly, and in a limited way, we can thrust the body out into space. But remember, nothing in this human body is designed to be permanent. However, God has designed a resurrection body that is going to be permanent, and in this resurrection body, we are going to be a part of God's ultimate triumph.

Psalm 110:1: "The Lord said unto my Lord, sit thou at my right hand, until I make thine enemies thy footstool." So we read "it is manifest that he is expected." "He" here refers to God the Father. We know that everything else is put under the Lord Jesus, but the Father isn't. A planner must be in the position that his plan is constantly under his control. And God's plan, which involves free will in man and free will in angels, must be perfect in every minute detail. God keeps control of that plan and never loses control of it. Born-again man ultimately inherits a resurrection body, without an old sin nature, minus human good, and perfect for all eternity. The unbeliever, on the other hand, has a resurrection body in which he will suffer for all eternity. So there are two resurrections. (Revelation 20) "Blessed is he that hath part in the first resurrection." And there are two kinds of resurrection bodies; those that can travel in space, and those that are designed to spend eternity in the lake of fire.

Next we read that "The Son is subject unto God." It is a "future tense" and this means a logical progression. It is middle voice and is reflexive, which refers to the humanity of Christ. His deity is co-equal with God. Then it says, "That **God** may be all in all" and God here refers to God the Father, God the Son, and God the Holy Spirit. The humanity of Jesus fits in the perfect plan of God. "All in all" means God will completely dominate in all eternity.

The plan was designed in eternity past, but the plan will be executed in eternity future. The resurrection body is designed to enjoy the future with God, a future that is not completely and adequately described anywhere in all the Bible. The resurrection body is designed to last through all eternity. It is designed to survive the nuclear destruction of the heavens and the earth.

Paul was trying to persuade the Greeks about the resurrection, so let's now move from eternity and come back into time and look at an argument that proves resurrection. Of course, you know that people were baptized in the first century, people like the Ethiopian Eunuch and the Philippian Jailer. All these people died, and when they died, other people were born, and as each generation came, those people were baptized. So we have been born twice and have been baptized twice, baptized in water and by the Holy Spirit. Baptism itself is an emphasis on the resurrection. Now this verse has not been correctly translated. Look at it for a moment just as it is.

1 Corinthians 15:29: "Else what shall they do which are baptized for the dead, if the dead rise not at all? Why are they then baptized for the dead?" Many people, like the Mormons for example, take this verse to mean that people should be baptized for the dead. The word "since" is a better translation than the word "else." "What shall they do" is a future, active, indicative of **poieo.** "Who are baptized" is a present, passive participle of **baptizo** and means to identify. The ritual of water baptism has been perpetuated through all the centuries. Millions and millions have been baptized. Baptism

as a ritual has been perpetuated in the church. The passive voice means that the one being baptized receives baptism as a testimony of resurrection.

The Significance Of Baptism

1. In baptism we are identified with Christ as he hung on the cross and bore our sins. This is retroactive positional truth.
2. Next, we are identified with Christ as he was raised up and was seated at the right hand of God.
3. Finally, in baptism we are identified with Christ in his death and his resurrection.

"For the dead" is **huper** plus the genetive and it doesn't mean "For the dead" but it means "In place of the dead, or instead of the dead." They are dead and can't be baptized again, but now you are living and you are to be baptized instead of them. You will die and others will be born, will believe, and they will come and will be baptized instead of you. So the ritual of baptism has been perpetuated for 2,000 years, and every time someone is baptized, it illustrates the truth of resurrection. "For the dead" is literally "in place of the dead."

"For The Dead" Should Read "In Place Of The Dead"

1. Why do believers in each generation observe the ordinance of baptism?
2. If there were no resurrection from the dead, then water baptism would be meaningless and would be discontinued.
3. Water baptism signifies our resurrection from the dead and our union with Christ.
4. If there had been no resurrection, water baptism would have been discontinued. Then Hellenistic culture would be right and the Bible wrong. Every generation that continues baptism is just another vindication of the truth of the bodily resurrection of Jesus Christ.

Now the Greeks rejected resurrection, but they were great lovers of form and ritual, so they quickly latched onto baptism in water. So Paul in substance here is saying, "Why are you Greeks baptizing if you don't believe in resurrection?" "If" the dead rise not is used here as a debater's first class condition. Paul assumes that the dead rise not in order to prove that they do arise from the dead. If there is no resurrection, then why do they keep on baptizing century after century?

The principle is this — Water baptism is perpetuated and does not die out from one generation to the next. It goes on and on and will go on to the end of time. Water baptism will continue as a ritual until the end of time, or rather the end of the Church Age. It has been ridiculed in every generation, and people have tried to make something out of it not intended by the Lord. Yet, baptism has continued in every generation, and even though people distort it, that doesn't destroy it. It continues just as Jesus commanded it. Jesus said, "Baptize them," and it is a command. People who do not stay with the Bible distort the issue and distort baptism. We have baptismal regeneration or spirituality by baptism. But this little word, **huper,** makes this verse clear and **huper** plus the genetive simply says, "People die and then another generation comes on the scene, and they are baptized just like those people who have died in the last generation were. Baptism continues from generation to generation because it portrays the death and resurrection of Christ." One of the results of the resurrection is the ritual of baptism century after century. The one thing this verse does not say is that a living person can be baptized in the place of a person already dead.

Down in verse 32 Paul refers to fighting wild animals in the arena at Ephesus. Now did Paul do this? No. His life was in danger at all times when he was in Ephesus. In Ephesus the gladiators fought the wild beasts in the arena. Later they found that Christians made great bait for wild animals, and they then threw Christians to the wild animals. Paul here is just assuming something for argument's sake. Paul is simply using a figure to show that he was in danger daily. So Paul is saying something like this — "Let's assume for the sake of argument that I fought with the wild beasts in Ephesus." Now he hadn't, but he was assuming that he had just to prove a point. When Paul wrote to the Corinthians, they were not yet throwing Christians into the arena for the wild animals to destroy. That came some years later.

1 Corinthians 15:30: "And why stand we in jeopardy every hour?" Paul is saying this. If there is no resurrection, then why go through all this struggle? Why suffer hardships and privations for the Gospel, if there be no resurrection? There is no reason to live under the pressure of the angelic conflict if there be no resurrection. In other words, no resurrection, no angelic conflict. If operation footstool is not true, then no resurrection. But the resurrection is true. It is an historical event. Christ couldn't be sitting at the right hand of God if he hadn't risen from the dead. But his humanity was resurrected, and he ascended and was seated at the right hand of God. Paul described his sufferings and stonings and privations in many other passages. But jeopardy is angelic pressure, unseen pressure. Paul is saying in substance this — "If there were no resurrection, then I would kick over the traces and give up the battle. But the resurrection that is coming holds me in line and keeps me on the right road."

1 Corinthians 15:31: "I protest by your rejoicing which I have in Christ Jesus our Lord, I die daily." "I protest" really means "I take a solemn oath." It is as when we sometimes say, "I swear to this with my hand on the Bible." "By your rejoicing" is a proof of the reality of the resurrection. Paul and these early Christians had inner happiness and inner peace, and this proved the reality of the coming resurrection.

1 Corinthians 15:32: "If after the manner of men I have fought with

beasts at Ephesus, what advantageth it me, if the dead rise not? let us eat and drink; for tomorrow we die." Here is another debater's first class condition. They all knew about the gladiators in the arena at Ephesus. Quite often those gladiators were slain by these wild animals. He is assuming this had happened to him just to make a point. So he says something like this — "If according to the standard of the day, I have fought with wild beasts in the arena at Ephesus, what advantage would that be to me if there is no resurrection?"

In other words, Paul was saying, "If there be no resurrection, am I wasting my time!" Paul is saying something like this — "If there be no resurrection, then I might as well have a fling and live it up. I'd eat and drink and live like a dog and then die and that's all there would be to it, if there were no resurrection. In other words, how do you explain the ability of Christians to stand up against the terrible pressures apart from the blessed hope of the resurrection?"

1 Corinthians 15:33-34: "Be not deceived: evil communications corrupt good manners. Awake to righteousness, and sin not; for some have not the knowledge of God: I speak this to your shame." Paul was reminding them not to be led astray by evil companions. These Greeks had evil companions who were leading them astray. Leading them astray with Hellenistic rationalism and false philosophies. They were being influenced with false philosophies. They were being influenced with false intellectualism. Paul says, "Stop being deceived by these people." "Evil companions" here in this passage refers to people who had rejected Bible doctrine and wanted to substitute philosophical concepts instead. They were warned that they should recover from a spiritual hangover.

WHAT KIND OF BODY WILL YOU HAVE IN THE RESURRECTION?

1 Corinthians 15:33: "Be not deceived: evil communications corrupt good manners." The words "Be not deceived" are present, active, imperative plus the negative and should read, "Stop being deceived." The Hellenistic culture inherited by the Greeks from the teaching of Plato and Aristotle had led them to reject bodily resurrection. They believed that every human being would die and that his soul would survive in a very happy place. Because of their training, they had been led to believe that there was something essentially evil about the body and that if a person could just get rid of his body, he would be much better off. They failed to understand the real meaning of the glory of the resurrection as presented by Christ and the New Testament. Many people are misled by their culture or by their friends and many times when your friends don't know doctrine, they can mislead you easily. Doctrine is just as necessary for the spiritual life as breathing is for the physical life. Legalism and the lack of exposure to doctrine causes people to accept unacceptable non-biblical views, and when people don't know Bible doctrine, they always look for some substitute. Rejection of the resurrection leads to the doctrine of eat, drink and be merry, and this is called **HEDO-NISM.** This is what the Greeks called it. Rejection of the resurrection always leads to some form of sublimation. They had people in the Corinthian Church, just as we have today, who refuse to learn Bible doctrine. These people do not understand the importance of the Bible. They are negative toward Bible doctrine, and this creates a vacuum in the soul and a vacuum in the mind. Into that vacuum comes legalism, religion, and an emphasis on the details of life. So the Corinthians, not knowing doctrine, had accepted the false system of Hedonism. If you don't believe in the resurrection, you might as well live it up and get all the pleasure you can out of this life, for you won't have a chance to get any pleasure out of the life to come.

1. People who reject doctrine are constantly looking for some form of pleasure and happiness apart from doctrine.
2. People are influenced by those with whom they associate. If you associate with those who reject Bible doctrine, it won't be long until you reject doctrine yourself. You become like those with whom you run.

So verse 33 begins with a command "Stop being deceived." The next words "evil communications" should be translated "evil companions." It doesn't mean immoral or wicked companions, but simply companions who reject Bible doctrine. The reason they are evil companions is that they reject Bible doctrine and influence others to reject it. The principle is set forth in Matthew 4:4. "But he answered and said, It is written, Man shall not live by bread alone, but by every word that proceedeth out of the mouth of God."

This means that Bible doctrine must stand first in a person's life. "They corrupt good usage" is a much better translation here. Manners are important, but these are not the words here. So this sentence should read, "Evil companions corrupt good application." One of the greatest hindrances to knowing doctrine is other people who don't think doctrine is important, for if you associate with them, they will eventually persuade you that doctrine is not important. You as a Christian are to shun people who downgrade doctrine. You become like those with whom you associate.

1 Corinthians 15:34: "Awake to righteousness, and sin not; for some have not the knowledge of God: I speak this to your shame." Here is a solution. It begins with the words "Wake up." But the word here is never used with waking up. The word used here really means "Sober up." This word is used here in a spiritual sense. It means you have been drunk because you are not interested in Bible doctrine, and Paul is telling them to sober up from their doctrinal indifference.

Up in the previous verse we saw that these Christians got very friendly with the crowd not interested in Bible doctrine and they became drunk on that kind of friendship. This put them on negative volition toward doctrine and will lead them to adopt a Hedonistic philosophy. They adopted as their mode of living pleasure, friends, loved ones, sex, details of life — things which always lead to the intensification of misery if Bible doctrine is neglected. So Paul here tells the Corinthians to sober up to Bible doctrine. The Word of God stored away in the mind is the only way you can be prepared for an emergency or a crisis. Friends will not carry you through pressure. Pleasure, sex, the details of life will not carry you. Only Bible doctrine in your mind will carry you. When you exclude Bible doctrine, you are on a spiritual drunk. So Paul says here "Sober up!"

The first thing you do when you sober up, you look at what you thought was that beautiful doll and you say, "What in the world am I doing with her?" And so it is with every other detail of your life. You look at pleasure and sex and the details of life and you say, "What are these things really doing to me?" Bible doctrine must be first, and when it is first, then everything else falls into its proper place. Paul reminded the Corinthians that evil associates lead you away from Bible doctrine. People who do not have Bible doctrine substitute something else for it. "Sober up" means to get away from those things which offer a weak substitute. This is between you and the Lord, so look at your habits, look at your way of thinking, and say to yourself, "What is the most important thing in my life?" Is it Bible doctrine or is it something

94

else? The Bible is the mind of Christ, and you've got to have his mind guiding your thinking if you are going to be happy. You can really begin to enjoy the details of life if Bible doctrine comes first in your life.

Quite often evil companions are those fine Christians who say to you, "Now you don't need all that Bible doctrine. You already know more than you apply. Come go with me and we'll have a better time over here than you will have in Bible class." "If the written word is first, then the Living Word is first." You can't put Christ first in your life until you put the written word first. There is no loving God and Christ apart from loving the word. Now you can be caught up in maudlin sentimentality which you call love, but it won't stand up when that first little bit of pressure comes on you. If you want to look into the mind of Christ and know his thoughts, then learn Bible doctrine. You pick out friends who put the word first and they are friends who are safe for you. Bible doctrine will make a marriage, not destroy it.

The people in Corinth were stupid. We will see that word used down in verse 36. One event of happiness after the other is not enough in the day to day rat race in order to keep you stable. But Bible doctrine will carry you through any catastrophe, and will stabilize you when nothing else will. Bible doctrine stabilized Jesus on the cross and when all else forsook him, including God the Father and God the Holy Spirit, the one thing that was adequate for the crisis was Bible doctrine.

They were to sober up to righteousness. They were to rebound as taught in Hebrews 6. After rebound they were to get Bible doctrine. "To righteousness" does not mean living a clean life, but is a technical term referring to the knowledge of doctrine plus the filling of the Holy Spirit, and this equals the production of divine good. This is the way for a Christian to sober up. Recover from the ignorance of Bible doctrine. And "Sin not" means that you are not to let sin keep you from learning the Bible. It is a present, active, imperative, and this means that this is a command from the Lord. Now we come to some questions concerning the resurrection.

1 Corinthians 15:35: "But some man will say, How are the dead raised up and with what body do they come?" The first question, "How are the dead raised up" has to do with the mechanics of the resurrection. This will be answered in verse 36. The second question will be answered in verses 37-49.

1 Corinthians 15:36: "Thou fool, that which thou sowest is not quickened except it die:" The word **Aphron** can best be translated by the word "stupid." It means "Not thinking." This means someone who can learn, but won't put forth the effort to do so. The stupid one here means the one who has the opportunity to learn doctrine but won't take advantage of it.

Since those being addressed lived in an agricultural economy, Paul here used an illustration they would readily understand. The seed looks one way when it is put in the ground, but it doesn't look that way when it comes up. The same way with the body. The body looks one way when you put it in the ground, but it looks another way when it is raised up. The seed was planted, and it died and became something else. When you die you will get a new form, a new kind of body. Your body that goes into the grave is one kind of body, and your body that comes out of the grave is another kind of body. Now Paul gives three illustrations.

1 Corinthians 15:37: "And that which thou sowest, thou sowest not that body that shall be, but bare grain, it may chance of wheat, or of some other grain." When you plant the seed in the ground, it is one kind of seed, and will be a different looking kind of thing when it comes up. It enters the ground a body of corruption, it comes out of the ground a body of incorruption.

1 Corinthians 15:38: "But God giveth it a body as it hath pleased him, and to every seed his own body."

God is the one who gives him a body as it is pleasing to him. Every seed has a different body. People recognize you here and when you are raised up, people will recognize you then. (I have a picture of my father and he has beautiful hair. Well, I never knew him when he had beautiful hair. But I would know that face anywhere. That's the way it will be when we see our loved ones in a resurrection body. It will be easier to recognize them up there than it is here.)

1 Corinthians 15:39: "All flesh is not the same flesh: but there is one kind of flesh of men, another flesh of beasts, another of fishes, and another of birds." Here is a second illustration and it is from animal life. All flesh is not the same flesh. You see, you cannot transmute from one flesh into another flesh. Walls separate the species of creation. Man didn't start out in one lower species and then evolve to something higher. Here are categories. I've seen some real good human species that were good arguments for evolution. There are some apes that look like men and some men that look like — and I'll leave that sentence right there.

Now there is a variation within a species, as in the case of dogs. There are many kinds of dogs, but dogs can't pass over into another species. You don't see dogs becoming human beings, or vice versa.

1. There is one flesh of men.
2. There is one flesh of beasts.
3. There is one flesh of fish.
4. There is one flesh of birds.

This may be the Bible's best answer to the theory of evolution. God is capable of keeping you and is capable of producing your resurrection body. We all have differences, and God will preserve those variations in our resurrection bodies. It will be easier to recognize someone in heaven in a resurrection body than it is to recognize him down here. Down here you haven't seen someone in many years and you say, "Why, I hardly recognized you!" But it won't be that way up there. You will have a perfect memory and perfect vision and you will easily recognize them there.

1 Corinthians 15:40-41: "There are also celestial bodies, and bodies terrestrial: but the glory of the celestial is one, and the glory of the terrestrial is another. There is one glory of the sun, and another glory of the moon, and another glory of the stars: for one star differs from another star in glory." Here we have a contrast of the resurrection body and the earthly body. The glory of the resurrection body is greater than the glory of the earthly body. The celestial, heavenly body has one glory. The terrestial body, which is the earthly body, has another glory.

In verse 41 he refers to the glory of the sun. The sun is the light bearer and gives light to all other objects. The moon reflects the light of the sun. The woman is most glorious when she reflects the light of the man. One is a light bearer and the other is a light reflector. One star differs from another, but they all have a glory. Each retains its identification. The difference in glory will be the difference in the reward.

XVI

AMAZING RESURRECTION CONTRASTS

Anyone who has ever studied anatomy or anything to do with the function of the human body, knows that the function of the human body is a most fantastic operation. There is nothing more amazing in the world than the function of the human body. The structure of the human body and its ability to cope with so many problems and to function under so many varied circumstances is truly one of the most astounding things in human history. However, it becomes obvious to each of us as we live in a human body that the human body as we know it was not designed for permanence. People who lived before the flood lived for long periods of time, but after the flood it is quite rare to hear of anyone living more than 100 years in the human body. The human body, as the Scripture states, is a tent. This tent is designed to house something that is to live forever and that something we call the human soul.

John 3:36 divides all humanity into two groups; namely, those who will spend all eternity with God and those who will spend all eternity in the lake of fire. The Lord Jesus Christ has made it possible for every human being in the earth to spend all eternity with God in Heaven. This they can do through an act of faith. "Believe on the Lord Jesus Christ and thou shalt be saved." But those who do not believe will not be saved, and will spend eternity separated from God.

The human body has amazed us throughout all history. It is amazing what the human body can take and yet live. Once the human body ceases to function the soul can no longer remain in the human body, and the soul departs the human body and moves into eternity. The human body is not designed to care for a life that is too long prolonged. Now this fact tells us a number of things. We do not possess a human body like the one Adam possessed when he came into the world. Adam lived for 930 years. This indicates to us that he had a fantastic instrument called the human body. His body was much greater and stronger than anything we know in human bodies today. In the time of Adam we also have Methuselah who lived almost 1,000 years. In fact, he broke Adam's record by a few years. Now this tells us that the human body, prior to the flood, was much greater than anything we know today. Today when people live a long time quite often their minds do not keep pace with their bodies.

In the passage we have before us now, we see the function of the human body being discontinued and the contrasts of the body of corruption. This body we have now that will last not more than 100 years is a body of corruption, and the body we will have in the future is a body of incorruption and it will last for eternity. Now there are two kinds of resurrection bodies of the future. There is the resurrection body of the believer, and the resurrection body of the unbeliever. The body of the unbeliever will come forth in the resurrection and this is called the second resurrection. These resurrected unbelievers will stand before Christ at the great white judgment throne to be sentenced to the lake of fire. These bodies will be capable of pain suffered from the burning fire but they will last forever and forever. Now that is not the same kind of body the believer will possess. The believer will participate in what is called "The first resurrection." We are now talking about the bodies of all those who believe in the Lord Jesus Christ. With the exception of the rapture generation, these will go through something about like this — All believers who have died physically, had a time when they were alive. At the time of their living they accepted Jesus Christ as Saviour, and at that point they entered into phase one of the plan of God, which we call salvation. Then they entered phase two of the plan, which we call the living of the Christian life. In this period they experienced what we call "living grace." Then at the end of that period they experienced "dying grace" and they moved into phase three of the plan, which we call eternity. During dying grace plans were completed for the soul to leave the body. The soul and human spirit, at the second of death, leave the body and for a time exist apart from a human body. The functions of the soul are such that the soul and the human spirit can exist without the aid of a human body. Mentality and reality exist without the aid of a human body. Now while on this earth the soul and human spirit can't exist without the aid of a human body. But once the human body dies, the soul then moves into the presence of God and functions without the aid of a human body. In this function of the soul and human spirit, there is perception without the help of a physical body. But this is only temporary and will continue only until the body of Christ is completed and the Angelic Conflict is finished. One generation will not see death and this is what we call "The Rapture." The souls and spirits already in Heaven will come with the Lord and meet in the air and those who are alive on the earth will go up.

1 Thessalonians 4:16-17: "For the Lord himself shall descend from heaven with a shout, with the voice of the archangel, and with the trump of God: and the dead in Christ shall rise first: Then we which are alive and remain shall be caught up together with them in the clouds to meet the Lord in the air: and so shall we ever be with the Lord." The Lord Jesus Christ will descend with his own and the "dead in Christ," which refers to the souls of these people will come back to earth and pick up a resurrection body and go

100

up first. Then those that are alive shall be caught up and will be given a resurrection body. The believer has a body of corruption during his lifetime. This body of corruption eventually leads to his death physically, unless the rapture occurs first. At death the body of corruption is set aside, and it disintegrates and returns to the elements from which it was originally made.

It is quite interesting how in wartime we give so much emphasis to the human body. We attempt to get back the bodies of every soldier killed on any battlefield so we can bury that body in the homeland. Our enemies know the value we place on a human body and they quite often shoot our soldiers as they go out and try to retrieve human bodies that have been shot down. The real person has already left that body, the soul is already gone, and that dead human body is not the real person. Once the soul leaves the body, it is not too important as to how that body ends up. Resurrection of the body can take place from anywhere, even if that body has rotted on a battlefield or been blown to bits or has been decomposed in the salty waters of the ocean.

An empty house is a good description of the dead body, for the real person has already departed. In the resurrection body, we will have something that is absolutely fantastic. It will never wear out. It will never grow old. It will withstand the destruction of what is now the heavens and the earth. There is no pressure so great that the resurrection body can be disturbed in any way.

We have come to a passage now which demands that, if we understand the passage, we must have all this doctrine in our minds. This passage is going to give us a contrast of the physical body and the resurrection body. This body we live in here on the earth in this passage is called the body of corruption. In another verse later on it will be referred to as a mortal body. Then later on it will be referred to as a corrupt body taking on incorruption. This refers to those who have died and their bodies have disintegrated. But there is one generation at the time of the rapture who have not died, so they are referred to as "mortal bodies" and they will become immortal. Immortality and incorruption refer to exactly the same results, one referring to the dead, the other referring to those who didn't die but were taken up in the rapture. No one should be afraid of death if he is a believer. Paul said, "To me to live is Christ, and to die is gain." Phil. 1:21. Fear of death is totally foreign to the Christian faith. Mature Christianity guarantees that you will not fear death. The 7,000 promises in the Bible are given to be used by us while we live in this body of corruption, and we are never to be afraid. Here in this passage before us we have contrasts outlined.

Eight Contrasts Concerning The Dead

1 Corinthians 15:42: "So also is the resurrection of the dead. It is sown in corruption; it is raised in incorruption."

Number 1

It is sown in corruption, and this means physical death. The physical body is destroyed by physical death. Incorruption means indestructible, and this is the body we will get in the resurrection. It cannot be destroyed. One is the body we have in time; the other is the body we will have in eternity. The body in time will be destroyed. The body in the resurrection has moved into eternity and nothing can destroy it or harm it in any way. Adam is the only man who ever experienced spiritual death while he was physically alive. When Adam sinned he immediately died spiritually, then about 1,000 years later he died physically. But we were born spiritually dead, we didn't have to wait and get that way like Adam did. The difference between us and Adam is this: we were born spiritually dead and Adam became spiritually dead when he ate of the forbidden fruit.

1 Corinthians 15:43: "It is sown in dishonour; it is raised in glory: it is sown in weakness; it is raised in power."

Number 2

"It is sown in dishonour" is a reference to the old sin nature, a reference to the thing which is wrong with the whole human race. This means exactly the same as the phrase, "As in Adam all die." Then the phrase, "It is raised in glory" refers to a new body without the old sin nature. So the old sin nature is the culprit and hence the real problem. When we are raised up we will have bodies minus the old sin nature. The old sin nature must be restrained in many ways. It must be restrained by common law, thus we have laws telling us what we can and cannot do. And as a deterent to crime we are given capital punishment. This is found in Genesis 9:6 and in Romans 13:4. The only way you can stop the criminal is by means of capital punishment. You cannot have an orderly society without capital punishment. So the words, "raised in glory," means to be raised up without an old sin nature. This is why it is said that when we see Christ we will be like him, and being like him means we will have no old sin nature, and will therefore produce no human good, only divine good.

Number 3

"It is sown in weakness." This refers to the fading nature of our physical bodies. The older we get the weaker we get and eventually we will have to be helped to get around if we live long enough. But when we are raised up we are no longer subject to our physical weaknesses. Time will not be a factor in our resurrection bodies.

1 Corinthians 15:44: "It is sown a natural body; it is raised a spiritual body. There is a natural body, and there is a spiritual body."

Number 4

The words, "It is sown a natural body," really mean a "soulish body" and is from **psuchikos**. It is called a soulish body because it houses the soul. It is often called "the natural man." This means that it is incapable of having

102

fellowship with God. When we are born again we get a human spirit and this means we can have fellowship with God. It is raised a **pneumatikos** body and this means a human body with a spirit. We are born in a body that cannot have fellowship with God, and we are raised in a body that can have fellowship with God.

1 Corinthians 15:45: "And so it is written, The first man Adam was made a living soul; the last Adam was made a quickening spirit."

Number 5

"So it is written" — and this is a perfect, passive, indicative and it means written in the past and it stands written forever. This is a quotation from Genesis 2:7, "The first man Adam" became **(ginomai)** a living soul. "The last Adam became a constantly giving life spirit." Here is now a contrast of positions and this refers to verses 20-22 of this chapter. We are all born physically alive but spiritually dead. We are all born in the first Adam. The words, "the last Adam," refer to Christ. The word "quickening" is a present, active, participle and means "a force constantly giving life." So this verse is a statement of the new birth. We are born spiritually dead, then we meet Christ and place our faith in him and are born again and become spiritually alive. We are born in a body headed for physical death, but in the resurrection we pick up a body that is headed for eternal spiritual life.

1 Corinthians 15:46: "Howbeit that was not first which is spiritual, but that which is natural; and afterward that which is spiritual."

Number 6

Here we have come to a contrast between the natural and the spiritual, and this brings the angelic conflict into view.

1. Man was created lower than angels and when man sinned he went lower down than that. By union with Christ we become higher than angels.

    Hebrews 1:13: "But to which of the angels said he at any time, Sit on my right hand, until I make thine enemies thy footstool?"

2. We who are "lower than lower" will become "higher than higher." Once we believe in Christ, positionally we are in union with Christ and thus are higher than angels and therefore subject to their attack.

3. Through death and resurrection of the last Adam, we are transferred to a higher sphere of life.

4. The seed must fall into the ground and die before it becomes a plant. Christ had to die in order for us to become "plants," in order for us to have resurrection bodies. The cross makes the resurrection possible.

5. It is in resurrection bodies that the church returns with Christ to put an end to the angelic conflict.

6. In this verse there is no verb and this means this is a verse of fantastic emphasis.

    We will eventually have in reality what we now have only potentially.